ROBIN LAING is a musician and writer, originally from Edinburgh, now based in South Lanarkshire. He is the author of four books on the subject of whisky and has released eight albums of whisky songs, as well as five albums of songs on various other subjects. He performs internationally as a singer-songwriter and is also chair of the tasting panel for the Scotch Malt Whisky Society. This publication is a departure for him – poems instead of songs and castles instead of whisky.

www.robinlaing.com

CW00901549

Books by the same author:

The Whisky Muse, Luath Press, 2002
The Whisky River, Luath Press, 2007
Whisky Legends of Islay, Luath Press, 2009
The Whisky Muse volume 2, Luath Press, 2018

The Queen's Bahookie

and other tales from Scotland's castles

ROBIN LAING

Luath Press Limited

EDINBURGH

www.luath.co.uk

First published 2024

ISBN: 978-180425-136-2

The author's right to be identified as author of this book
under the Copyright, Designs and Patents Act 1988 has been asserted.

Printed and bound by
Clays Ltd., Bungay

Typeset in 10.5 point Mrs Eaves OT by
Main Point Books, Edinburgh

Illustrations © Bob Dewar 2024
Text © Robin Laing 2024

Contents

CONTENTS

INTRODUCTION

STRANGELY, PERHAPS, I find that old, ruined castles fire and inspire my imagination more than the still occupied sort – maybe I have some kind of affinity with their dilapidated, well-past-their-best state of repair. For this project I travelled around Scotland visiting castles which are under the protection of Historic Environment Scotland; I wanted to get good use out of my Life Membership before it lapsed.

Some of these sites are blissfully peaceful; you can enjoy the landscape, the natural environment and the views, you can appreciate the once impressive (sometimes still impressive) architecture and reflect on days gone by and ways of living, surviving and managing affairs that were so different from what we experience now.

Some people visit these places with a camera – I took my notebook. All visitors are probably touched by the other-worldliness of Scotland's crumbling castles. Crumbling they may be, but they were built to be strong and so they have survived the ravages of time better than most of their contemporary structures.

They were built to be strong for good reason – to repel attack, to protect inhabitants and to show the power of their owners – and so are fundamentally expressions of people's ambitions or insecurities in times of conflict and turbulence. The stones may now bear the lichens of age, the patina of centuries and the erosion of weather, but in their dumb vibrations are found countless tales of past dramas and deeds of derring-do, treachery, bravery, misfortune, allegiances, privation, punishment and reward. Listen more closely and there are hints of love and loyalty, personal joys and sufferings and even minute details of domestic activities and procedures.

I planned to visit a few castles and to write at least three poems inspired by each. In fact, I visited 21 and thoroughly enjoyed seeing so many parts of the country, some fairly unfamiliar to me, drinking in the atmosphere, touching and listening to the stones and picking up fragments of historical tales, in some cases wondering how to retell them and in others imagining how to fill the gaps. I have tried not to play too fast and loose with historical facts, but it is sometimes difficult to be absolutely sure of the ground when peering through the mists of time and gleaning scraps of information from a variety of sources. If my approach to history is more like that of Shakespeare or Hollywood I make no apology. I am writing poetry for entertainment, not as research or academic analysis. It is the 'story' part of history that fascinates me most. The bedrock of these musings might be things that actually happened but much of the landscape on top is formed from my imagination.

Working on this project has undoubtedly given me a deeper understanding of our country's past and a heightened awareness of how life might have been in previous ages, before industrialisation and urbanisation, before peace and democracy and before central heating, electric ovens and flushing toilets. I hope that these poetic musings and playful observations will give you a fraction of the pleasure that I got from visiting these sites.

BALVENIE

I HAVE VISITED Balvenie Castle on a number of occasions; it stands in Dufftown in the heart of Speyside and I have often found myself in that area because of my whisky interests (and of course for other reasons too). I have even attended an event in the castle as part of the Spirit of Speyside whisky festival. The castle overlooks William Grant's Glenfiddich distillery and in the grounds of the Glenfiddich complex is also to be found Balvenie distillery, which obviously takes its name from the castle. The Balvenie has a fine reputation as a single malt; indeed, the final line of my 'Speyside Whisky Song' proclaims that 'Balvenie is Viagra in a glass!' though that may involve a tiny hint of poetic licence.

The original castle was built in the 13th century by the 'Black Comyns', Earls of Buchan. In 1306 Robert the Bruce murdered John Comyn (though he was a Red, rather than a Black Comyn) in Greyfriars church in Dumfries and that was pretty much the end of their tenure. For the first half of the 15th century, the castle was owned by the 'Black Douglases' until James II rid himself of that lot

between the infamous Black Dinner in 1440 and the battle of Arkinholm in 1455. Soon after that, he entrusted Balvenie to a kinsman, John Stewart, Earl of Atholl, and his wife Margaret (the Fair Maid of Galloway) for the required annual rent of one red rose, to be paid at the feast of the Nativity of Saint John the Baptist, which is more or less midsummer.

So all this pretty much explains my villanelle about 'Balvenie Castle and the Red Rose' and 'The Colourful History of Balvenie Castle'. 'Balvenie – Once Upon a Time' is a reflection on the stark difference between what the castle might have been like during its centuries of occupation (domestic bustle and political machinations) and the way it is now, visited by tourists (and poets) through the day and by wildlife at night. 'Balvenie Castle in May' was written when I was in the area for the Spirit of Speyside whisky festival. In early May the uplands of Moray can fluctuate rapidly between winter conditions and summer warmth. The 'woman spurred to suicide' refers to the local, 18th-century tale of Barbara McIntosh, who committed suicide after being abandoned by her husband. She was buried in unhallowed ground on the slopes of Ben Rinnes (which you can see from the castle) and on at least two occasions her remarkably well-preserved body was dug up by groups of men with ghoulish curiosity; she was eventually reinterred in an Aberlour graveyard, but that area on Ben Rinnes is still known as Babbie's Moss.

Balvenie Castle and the Red Rose

Our summer season comes but then it goes;
It pleases us to hear its joyful song
For few things lift the heart more than a rose.

Young James, the King of Scots, the legend goes,
Lived life in haste and did not reign for long;
Our summer season comes but then it goes.

In time he did prevail against his foes;
He said 'It is important to be strong,
But few things lift the heart more than a rose.'

The beauty of a woman sometimes glows
And such was Lady Margaret, wife of John;
Our summer season comes but then it goes.

The King gave them Balvenie and he chose
A rent of one red rose, paid at St John's,
For few things lift the heart more than a rose.

And now it can be hard to think of those
Who lived here at Balvenie, time long gone,
Our summer season comes but then it goes.

So when I'm feeling weighed by winter woes,
I see that rose, red at midsummer's dawn;
Our summer season comes and then it goes
But few things lift the heart more than a rose.

Balvenie
Once Upon a Time

The Colourful History
of Balvenie Castle

Once upon a time,
Lives were played out here.
People built this place.
Echoes in the stone.

Now that time is gone,
Tourists come instead,
Taking photographs,
Buying souvenirs –

Then when darkness falls,
Acrobatic bats
And shrieking barn owls come
To terrorise the night.

So the rhythm goes;
Days and nights rotate,
But not the way it was
Once upon a time.

Black Comyn
Fealty
Red Comyn
Rivalry
Greyfriars
Enmity
Black deeds
Villainy
Black Douglas
Dynasty
Red birthmark
Royalty
Black Dinner
Infamy
Red Rose
History.

Balvenie Castle in May

I stand before Balvenie's roofless walls,
The land is slowly waking up to Spring;
Some jackdaws bounce upon the gusting wind
Like papers threaded on elastic string.
Now shaken loose, a rain of blossom falls
And by a cloud of hail the sun is dimmed.
Then, far away, a sunbeam strikes the hills –
Ben Rinnes, with its ragged granite tors,
Shines brightly in a covering of snow,
Reminding me of half-forgotten tales;
A woman spurred to suicide, and wars
We fought for pointless causes long ago.
Wherever in this land you choose to go
You feel the past, its pull, its undertow.

BLACKNESS

JUTTING OUT INTO the Firth of Forth from its south shore, Blackness Castle has the shape of a ship about to be launched. It is sometimes referred to as 'the ship that never sailed' and its main buildings have nautical names: the 'main mast tower', the 'stem tower' and the 'stern tower'.

The first castle on this site dates from around 1440 and was significantly added to in two phases in the 1500s. Blackness originally belonged to the Crichton family, but was 'acquired' by James II in 1454 and from then on various keepers were appointed to look after the castle on behalf of the King. The remodelling and reinforcements done in the 1530s were carried out by Sir James Hamilton of Finnart, the Master of Works of James V. Hamilton of Finnart was also the builder of Craignethan Castle and that probably explains why both of these castles feature caponiers (a defensive construction involving a covered passage across a ditch).

It seems the Stewart kings seldom visited Blackness, however, and only James IV visited more than once. Nonetheless, the keepers would have been expected to always have the castle in a state of readiness for a royal visit. I imagined that on the very rare occasion of a visit by the King and Queen, the castle keeper would have made strenuous efforts to impress. In 1506 James IV was apparently entertained here by four minstrels playing on shawms (a medieval version of the oboe). This is the background to 'A Banquet Fit for a King', which also imagines the efforts that kitchen staff might have gone to in those days.

Blackness, like many other Scottish castles, has a rather scary dungeon. I have written about other prison pits if they have unusual features, and in this case the ground-level prison (reserved for low status prisoners) had no sanitation but, being below sea level, was 'slopped out' by the sea at each high tide; hence 'The Prison and the Pit'. In 1924 an iron manacle was discovered there which still held the wrist bones of some poor, long-dead prisoner. Blackness also hosted some rather high-status prisoners, including, for example, Cardinal David Beaton, Archbishop of St Andrews, in 1543.

Such prisoners would not have had to suffer the slopping out but would have had more comfortable guest apartments.

When I visited, the tour guide was proud to tell me of this castle's role in various films. It has quite possibly featured in more movies and TV dramas than any other castle in Scotland. Productions such as *Hamlet* (1990), *The Bruce* (1996), *Macbeth* (1997), *Ivanhoe* (1997), *Doomsday* (2008), *Outlander* Season 1 (2014), *The Outlaw King* (2018) and *Mary Queen of Scots* (2018) have all had scenes shot at this 'Movie Star Castle'.

The Prison and the Pit

Dear Lady, please don't be concerned for these
Poor wretches in the pit; though foul disease
Discomfort them and blight their worthless souls,
It is their lot to rot in stinking holes
Because of what they've done. They are the scum
Of the Earth; some are vile traitors and some
Have disrespected property or killed
Innocent victims on a whim; they're wild
And quite beyond rehabilitation.
I do understand your consternation,
But believe me they are not worth your care;
They lie there and twitch, like rats in a lair;
Two times each day they are washed by the sea,
But nothing can cleanse their iniquity.
In that stem of the ship that never sets
Sail, they cower like dogs; please do not fret,
Life is cheap to these swine, so let them lie,
Let them howl, let them weep, let them die – aye
Let them proceed to the torments of hell;
We'll see in which pit then they'd rather dwell.
Our hearts must be hard and deaf to their pleas,
Cold as the swell of the unending seas,
Aloof as a king on exalted throne,
Hard as the black basalt, sharp jutting stone
That they have as their bed, fixed as the law,
Free from concern as a predator's claw,
Firm as authority, stiff as the dead.

Life is secured by a very fine thread,
This we should know and remember it well
When we choose to do wrong; and truth to tell,
For justice to work we depend on fear
And few things can make the heart quail, my dear
Lady, than the thought of being immured
Down there – now, shall we proceed with the tour?

Movie Star Castle

You are a star – a movie star
That's what you are
No doubt about it,
You should be fed on caviar
And served champagne;
We should not whisper –
   we should shout it
Over and over and over again.

Blackness Castle
Your looks bedazzle,
Your location
Is a sheer sensation,
Any film-maker's gift;
And you're a star
Just as you are,
You don't need no CGI,
No facelift
Or cosmetic,
Other settings are pathetic
Compared to you.

They all apply
And join the queue
Whenever films are being made.
You put the others in the shade,
The bar is high,
You set the standard;
You face to seaward
And to landward,
Excellence your keyword.

Your rugged beauty
Would enhance
Any movie,
Period drama or romance;
Long may you reign,
Long may you prosper,
More valuable far than any popstar;
Let's start a campaign
To nominate you for an Oscar!

A Banquet Fit for a King

Such a fine banquet has never been seen
At Blackness Castle before:
We served the King well,
He was pleased, I could tell;
Both he and the Queen
Enjoyed our cuisine
And I hope they will visit us more.

For numerous days before the feast
We sent folk out – both west and east,
Far and wide on errands they roamed,
The countryside like a horse tail was combed,
They foraged and gathered from hedgerow and moor,
From forest and valley, from field and from shore;
The finest porkers and kye were brought
By tether and hoof; and birds were bought.
The King's rabbit warrens were practically emptied
And all the plump doves that were easily tempted
Were grabbed in the castle dovecot.
The fishermen all put on their warm coats
And took to the Forth – a flotilla of boats
With their nets and their pots
And their lines and their floats
To bring the sea's bounty to shore.
And so our small army
Went out on its journey
Whether the weather was fair or was stormy
To stockpile our kitchen and store.

The cooks did us proud,
For it tested their skill
With cauldron and grill,
With fires well-lit
Under oven and spit,
In the kitchen so hot
Full of steam from each pot,
All to fill such a bill
That in other days might have been thought
Overkill.
I can picture it yet,
The fret and upset
And the turnbrochie's sweat
Which was less from the heat
Than the master cook's threat
But all in the end came right and complete.

The feast we laid out
Was, without any doubt,
Fit for a king and a queen.
The tables were groaning under the weight
Of many a bowl and many a plate,
Platters and trays and turrines.
There was lobster and ling
And dark smoked herring
And oysters and cockles and prawns,
For the sea brings her bounty right to our door
And we harvest it well
On the tide and the swell;
But for this feast we had so much more –
There was oven-baked swan
With its feathers stuck on,
We had honey-roast quails
And slow-cooked oxtails,

Fancies and fritters and fruits,
A spit-roasted pig
With a cute cabbage wig
And its piglets were puddings in cloots.

There were pastries and pies
Of various sizes
And one was a tart
In the shape of Blackness,
A pure work of art
But the idea was mine I confess;

A fine calf's head
Was the star of the spread,
It was sweetly adorned
With a pale anadem
And a pole we had torn
From a twisted bay stem
So it looked like the horn
Of a fine unicorn
And to make it look white
We gave it a baste
Of wet flour paste.
I wouldn't have sworn
It was in the best taste,
But the King laughed out loud
So it turned out alright
And we all felt quite proud.

The mood in the hall was special that night
With roaring fires and soft tallow lights;
There were dancers clacking on wooden boards
And some that wore kilts leaping high over swords;
An old balladeer that tended to shout

And jugglers throwing fire about
(That performance was shock and awe)
But according to James
The best of the games
Was not the juggler juggling flames,
But four minstrels piping on shawms;
To me they sounded like tortured toms,
But the King was engrossed
And if he was happy as pigs in straw
Then that's what matters the most.

Such a fine banquet has never been seen
At Blackness Castle before,
We served the King well,
He was pleased, I could tell;
Both he and the Queen
Enjoyed our cuisine
And I hope they will visit us more.

BOTHWELL

BOTHWELL CASTLE IS only a short drive from where I live, so it is a site I visit quite regularly, usually when I have visitors and want to show them the local places of interest. For this series of poems, I visited with my youngest daughter who was then still at primary school, so some of the subjects are mildly playful, especially the triolets about 'Pigeons in the Donjon' and 'Trebuchet'.

The role of Bothwell Castle in the Wars of Independence fascinates me – how it was besieged and taken and then counter-attacked on a number of occasions; contemporaneous written accounts almost bring these events to life like an action movie. This inspired 'Bothwell Castle and the Wars of Independence'; I was particularly touched by the story of Sir Andrew Moray who recaptured the castle in 1337. Bothwell belonged to his family and yet he had to tear it down in line with the policy, initiated by Robert the Bruce, of making sure that strategic castles could no longer be held by the English. I found the booklet *Bothwell Castle* (written by Chris Tabraham for Historic Scotland) very helpful here and that is where some of the quotes come from.

One of the curious things that affected me most about Bothwell Castle was to see the foundations that were put in place for the next phase of construction. Events dictated that this final phase was never realised, but you could imagine building it up like some Minecraft citadel. The floor plan and an artist's impression of what the finished castle might have looked like (both are in the visitor guidebook) show that it would surely have been one of the great medieval castles of Europe. This is the thought that concludes the sonnet 'Visiting Bothwell Castle'.

Bothwell Castle
A Trio of Triolets

I

Blood-red Sandstone Walls

Here the setting autumn sun
Bathes these blood-red sandstone walls.
Now, before the day is done,
Hear the setting autumn sun
Speak of battles lost and won;
Sunsets snap – but time still crawls.
Now the setting autumn sun
Bathes these blood-red sandstone walls.

II

Trebuchet

I saw in vaulted storeroom here
A clutch of balls made out of stone;
I heard the creak of winding gear.
I saw in vaulted storeroom here
The soaring arc that sliced the air;
By trebuchet these balls were thrown.
I saw in vaulted storeroom here
A clutch of balls made out of stone.

III

Pigeons in the Donjon

We saw pigeons in the donjon
Acting like they owned the place;
One had been a raptor's luncheon.
We saw pigeons in the donjon
Weakness is by brute force bludgeoned,
That has always been the case;
We saw pigeons in the donjon
Acting like they owned the place.

Visiting Bothwell Castle

The river Clyde with endless flow runs by,
A partial frame for Bothwell Castle's walls.
Though shattered now, they speak of glory past
And still they seem to reach into the sky.
The donjon's sad destruction still appals
And shows that grace and beauty never last.
But what amazes me when I come here
To see the trace of Bothwell's early plan –
The soaring scale of that which might have been –
Whose walls and towers never did appear.
An artist's reconstruction shows the span,
The spread, the scope of buildings never seen;
So Bothwell Castle seems to mirror me:
The things I've done – and things that could not be.

Bothwell Castle and the Wars of Independence

In twelve ninety-six, Bothwell Castle fell
To Edward First, the Hammer of the Scots;
But not for long, for in a year the Scots
Prevailed against the foe at Stirling Bridge.
For fourteen months the castle they assailed
And once again the English were sent home.
But three years on, the English King was back.
Determined Bothwell Castle should be won,
He built a mighty engine for the siege
And brought it up from Glasgow to attack.
He built a bridge and then he built a road,
To place 'the belfry' up against the walls.
How many fell and died in that assault
We do not know, but Edward's army was
So huge, that Bothwell was again laid low.
And so in English hands for years it stayed –
Till Bannockburn and in that aftermath
Fitzgilbert wisely left the gates ajar.

Returning then in thirteen thirty-six
The English took the castle once again
And yet again they tried to take this land.
They say a hero comes to meet the hour:
Sir Andrew Moray was the man this time
And Bothwell was his great ancestral home.
He led the struggle to keep Scotland free
As others (like his father) had before;
Another engine came to lead the siege:
'The Bowstoure' laid against 'that stalwart toure'
Soon brought the English tenure to an end.

But Moray had to cast the donjon down
To keep the castle out of English hands
And Scotland never had a tower so fine;
To see it fall – it must have pained his heart.

CAERLAVEROCK

CAERLAVEROCK CASTLE, NEAR the Solway coast, is to my mind one of the most attractive of Scotland's many castles. It was built around 1220 by the Maxwell family. For me, its most defining features are its symmetrical, triangular shape, so striking in aerial photographs and floor plans, and its surviving moat. The beauty of its red sandstone walls is another of the reasons I have visited the castle on numerous occasions.

The aesthetic appeal of its design lies behind the 'Caerlaverock Castle' sonnet, while the impressive moat inspired my rather light-hearted piece, 'Caerlaverock Moat'. In that poem, I tried to enhance the humour of the subject matter with some frivolous word play, using as many half rhymes for moat as I could think of.

The position of this castle, so close to the border with England, meant that it frequently featured in the regular conflicts between Scotland and our larger neighbour to the south. The most famous occasion was the determined siege of 1300 by Edward I, 'Hammer of the Scots'. The siege was celebrated in a poem composed at the time by the victorious English army. With their recurring rivalries and conflicts, these two feuding nations are characterised in the Caerlaverock guidebook as 'The Thistle and the Rose', referring to the floral emblems of Scotland and England respectively – hence my reflections in the poem with that title.

Caerlaverock Castle

Caerlaverock Castle stands in its moat;
What a shape, what lines and what symmetry,
Like the rising prow of a sturdy boat
Its elegant, gracious geometry.
Trapezoid or triangle in its form,
A shield, or a fan, or a trebuchet;
Built to withstand military storms,
Yet it has art and displays great beauty;
Concentric circles of a tight defence
So balanced, contained, protected and strong,
With towers and walls imposing, immense;
Could any castle more deserve a song?
From soaring, inspired imagination,
A gem in the crown of this small nation.

Caerlaverock Moat

I saw a vessel on the moat.
A Lord and Lady there had met;
She hoped that he would not forget
A nice romantic day afloat.

She courted him with all her might
But he to love could not admit
And though her eyes with love were lit
He was a stern and sober knight.

She offered him both wine and meat
And tried to play the diplomat;
She smiled beneath her wide straw hat
But he would neither drink nor eat.

The waters lapped the castle motte;
She prattled on but he was mute,
Which led to tension and dispute
And soon untied their lovers' knot.

He said he could not be her mate
Because her face looked like a mutt;
Plus, she was too fat in the gut –
It hurt to call her overweight.

She said he was a callous brute;
He stood, which caused the boat to rock
So there beside Caerlaverock
She kicked his shin and pushed him oot.

The Thistle and the Rose

The bristly thistle and the rose
Could hardly ever, I suppose,
Be well-contented bedfellows:
They simply were not suited.
When the bitter north wind blows
The thistle takes it on the nose
And in its stony soil it grows
Secure and firmly rooted.

Thistles are not useful crops;
With jaggy leaves and spiky tops
They're seldom found in flower shops,
Unwelcome weeds, indeed;
Armed to the teeth like special ops,
Botanical triceratops
Only valued by the Scots,
Their enemies to impede.

But the rose – with petals soft and scented,
So beautiful and ornamented –
Surely for lovers was invented,
All elegance and grace;
The rose is lovely, smooth and splendid,
To look, to sniff – we all are tempted;
When day begins or when it's ended
It always has its place.

How could a flower so full of charm,
A bloom whose good looks so disarm
Ever cause you any harm?
But is it quite so sinless?
Cos don't forget it has a thorn,

An evil, hidden devil's horn;
Don't get too close – you have been warned
It could leave you skinless.

Each nation has its bloom or blossom,
Some are pretty, some are awesome,
Some are odd, even unwholesome,
But never accidental.
In what ways these two different flowers
Reflect their parent superpowers
Well, that could entertain for hours –
I am non-judgemental.

But the thistle's barb, it's safe to bet,
Is more defence and less a threat,
What you see is what you get,
No hidden complications;
The rose is never so straightforward,
You might not get what you thought you ordered
And when your chum becomes a warlord
You will feel consternation!

CASTLE CAMPBELL

CASTLE CAMPBELL IS a kind of hidden treasure, tucked away up Dollar Glen, waiting to be discovered. The guidebook describes its 'solemn and lofty isolation'; lofty it certainly is, as you will know if you walk up the path from Dollar. Two of the triolets were inspired by this loftiness, one after enjoying the first warm sun of the year in the castle garden (with a hot chocolate from the self-service café) while the other is a song of sympathy for the labourers who had to transport the building materials up that steep and winding road. The final triolet is about one of the castle's more famous visitors, John Knox, the fiery preacher and leader of the Protestant Reformation in Scotland in the 16th century.

There is something evocative and atmospheric about this castle and that is reflected somehow in the topography. When built, in the early 15th century, it was known as Castle Gloom. The name was changed when Colin Campbell, 1st Earl of Argyll, acquired the castle in 1488. On either side of Castle Gloom run the Burn of Sorrow and the Burn of Care, which converge below and tumble into Dollar (dolour?) Glen; these sound like made up names from some fairy tale. I combined these suggestions of sadness and despair with a reflection about the pit prison and who some of its unfortunate inhabitants might have been in 'Castle Gloom'.

There are countless tales of courtly intrigue and shifting allegiances in the castles I have visited, but the one from Castle Campbell is a stoater. Archibald Campbell, the 8th Earl, was made a marquis by Charles I in 1641, but he soon fell out with the King through his support for the Covenanters. After Charles I was executed, the Scots crowned Charles II at Scone in 1641 and it was Archibald that placed the crown on the head of the restored King, but then he promptly changed sides again. In 1661, Archibald was executed in Edinburgh by order of the King; yet another victim of the infamous 'Maiden', a small-scale guillotine which can still be seen in the National Museum of Scotland – hence 'Archibald and the Maiden'. I borrowed the metre of Tennyson's In Memoriam as it seems to suit the subject of the unhappy death of an important man.

Castle Gloom

Dolour Glen is fed by tears
That from the mountains fall,
Through ancient woods and hills of fern
Where mists hold all in thrall,

There swiftly flow the gurgling streams
Of Sorrow and of Care;
Dampness and the dripping dew
Hang heavy in the air.

And where the tall and shaded trees
Wave to the silver moon,
In eerie silhouette one sees
The shape of Castle Gloom.

The halls and rooms of Castle Gloom
Have seen bright fire and light,
But it's a sad and soulful tale
That whispers there tonight;

The gargoyle heads of waterspouts
Gaze bleakly from the tower
And overhead the grim Green Man
Recalls John Knox's glower.

All is quiet in Castle Gloom,
Not a room is lit,
But darkness broods most heavily
In the prison and the pit,

For in that dank and airless place
Where nothing lives or grows,
The ground contains faint traces
Of miseries and woes;

There may be blood, there will be tears,
There may be dust of bones,
There may be faded scratchings
Upon the greasy stones.

Distant cries of pain and fear,
Injustice or disgrace,
Of shamefulness and hopelessness
Still echo in this place.

Far from the sun, the trees, the air,
Forsaken and alone –
How could any soul survive
This wretched box of stone?

Archibald Campbell and the Maiden

The Maiden sits in Chambers Street
And tourists come to stand and stare;
This is no maiden fresh and fair,
But one with corpses at her feet.

Three times fifty souls have passed
Beneath her slicing, slanting blade
And though today she is displayed,
A curiosity from the past,

It is not hard to hear the cries,
To see that mechanism drop,
To feel the blade that severed hope
Under damp, doom-laden skies;

And Castle Campbell's fated laird
Died here in sixteen sixty-one,
His hand was played, his race was run
And on that bar his neck was bared.

The night before, they say he slept
And in the morning faced his fate;
The Maiden was an open gate
Through which his soul to Heaven leapt.

Of treason Campbell was accused
And guilty found when he was tried;
Between opposing, warring sides,
In truth, he found it hard to choose.

So when his reckoning came around
For lack of loyalty he paid
The price – to this bloodthirsty blade,
By order of the King he'd crowned.

Castle Campbell
Triolets

I

The View from Castle Campbell's Garden

From Castle Campbell's garden fair
We gazed across the countryside;
Without a care we sat and stared
In Castle Campbell's garden fair;
We felt so high above things there,
The distance deep, the vista wide,
From Castle Campbell's garden fair
We gazed across the countryside.

II

Castle-building Labourer's Song

Onwards and upwards at less than a crawl,
Oh, when will this toiling ever be done?
We carry the stone for Castle Gloom's walls
Onwards and upwards at less than a crawl;
Progress restrained by this long up-slope haul,
Shivered by showers or baked by the sun,
Onwards and upwards at less than a crawl,
Oh, when will this toiling ever be done?

III

John Knox's Pulpit

The man who once came here to preach
Had dangling sleeves and noble beard;
A light was in his eye – his speech
(The man who once came here to preach)
Was like surf crashing on the beach.
Our sinful, muddled heads were cleared
By him who once came here to preach
With dangling sleeves and noble beard.

CRAIGMILLAR

ALTHOUGH I WAS born and brought up in Edinburgh, I had never visited the inside of Craigmillar Castle until I started on this project. I am so glad now to have discovered how impressive it is. The castle was built in the 14th century by the Preston family, who were involved in various intrigues over the centuries, including the infamous murder of the Earl of Mar in 1479: he had his throat cut while taking a bath in a house in the Canongate.

In 1566, Mary Queen of Scots was invited to stay at Craigmillar by Sir Simon Preston, one of her loyal supporters. She had stayed there before in happier days, but this had been an *annus horribilis* for the Queen. Her marriage to Darnley had gone completely sour (it has been suggested that the plot to murder him was hatched during this stay at Craigmillar), her court favourite and confidant, David Rizzio, had been murdered in front of her at the Palace of Holyrood and she was probably suffering post-natal depression after the recent birth of her son, James. When she arrived at Craigmillar in November that year, she was in a very unhappy state and probably knew things were falling apart

– it would only be a few months until she was forced to abdicate and imprisoned in Lochleven Castle.

Craigmillar Castle has many attractive features and has provided the backdrop for a few movie scenes. I was particularly impressed by the two ancient yew trees that stand either side of the door in the inner courtyard (I recognised them in *The Outlaw King*) and wrote 'The Craigmillar Yews' as a tribute to them.

The inside of the castle, especially the tower house and the adjoining east range, is a bit of a warren of rooms, stairs, passageways and alcoves, which can be difficult to navigate on a first visit, but could be a perfect place for a game of hide and seek – I tried to catch this in the 'Hide and Seek' sonnet. Incidentally, the guide told me that Craigmillar was one of the few Scottish castles never to have been damaged or partially destroyed in armed conflict, which explains its fine state of preservation. The guidebook says it was besieged and taken by the English army in 1544 (part of the 'Rough Wooing'); perhaps Sir Simon Preston surrendered rather than have his fine castle suffer damage.

The Craigmillar Yews

Two yew trees with gnarled trunks
Stand sentry at the door.
Feng-shui-dragon-like they lurk,
Their branches claw the air.

These twisted, giant bonsai forms
Are such a sweet surprise,
Their bows and curtseys so disarm
We smile and whisper praise.

For generations now they've stood
Within the courtyard wall.
Much has gone, but they have stayed
To dumbly tell the tale

Of all the winters they have lived
Through wind and snow and ice
And how in summer stretched and strived
Towards the sun's warm face.

Songbirds come to eat their fruit
And make a merry noise;
Among the castle lines so straight
We love those twisted boughs.

Their branches can bring motion
And colour to this place;
Without their contribution
Our visit would be less.

We leave these doorpost sentinels
Nobly standing there
Wondering what parables
And symbols may be here;

Birth, death and resurrection,
A doorway to the past
And the bitter-sweet reflection
That nothing really lasts.

Mary Queen of Scots at Craigmillar Castle, 1566

She came here to escape the town,
The intrigues and affairs of state,
The endless quarrel and debate,
From time to time it got her down.

In this hall they would feast and dance
And play sweet music through the night,
Or tell their tales by candlelight
Of how things were before, in France.

Auld Reekie was a stifling place,
The closes smelled of rancid stew
And housewives yelling 'gardyloo' –
So hard to find a wholesome space;

But here there was a garden fair,
With birds and bees beside the pond,
With trees and little hills beyond
And herb and blossom scented air.

She had her palace home, it's true,
With wealth and comfort all around,
But peace of mind could not be found
And happy memories now were few;

But here she could find rest and ease:
She walked upon the roof at night
And saw the distant city lights
And felt the freshness of the breeze.

Now this year, as the autumn dies,
Before the winter settles in,
She comes with heavy heart and pain,
Without that sparkle in her eyes.

She had to watch her David fall,
Murdered in the supper room;
Since then, she cannot shake the gloom
That seems to wrap her like a shawl.

Perhaps if God would intervene
And foil the devils at her heels...
But this could be, she somehow feels,
The autumn of her days as Queen.

Hide and Seek

This castle, which has never heard the din
Of war, the thud of guns, the crash of stone,
Gives me instead the sounds of children calling.
In cubicles and cubbyholes they grin,
The perfect place for hide and seek (alone,
Yet not alone); they're running, climbing, crawling,
Counting, seeking, finding; they laugh and shriek.
Such higgledy-piggledy random walls,
And dark staircases (some lie side by side),
The nooks and crannies, places one might sneak;
In turrets and towers, cellars and all,
I hear those joyful echoes amplified
In stone. The castle seems so still today;
If I must choose – war or play – I choose play.

CRAIGNETHAN

THIS IS MY LOCAL castle and the one that started this project off. I live within walking distance of Craignethan and so I visit it frequently and got to know the custodian and some of the guides. I find this a very peaceful place; it is tucked away in a loop of the Nethan River, which joins the Clyde at Crossford, and because of its somewhat remote location, it perhaps gets fewer visitors than it deserves.

We like to visit Craignethan in the springtime, when it opens up after its winter season closure, and soon the site comes alive with swallows nesting in various places within the building and swooping endlessly across the courtyard lawn. This activity somehow conveys the essence of my favourite season, hopefully captured in 'Craignethan Swallows'.

I show the castle off to our house guests, we have family picnics there and sometimes it is just a refuge for quiet contemplation. It was during one of those moments of reflection that I started to think poetically about the walls. As much as I love the red sandstone castles of Caerlaverock, Bothwell and Urquhart, I find the honeyed hues of Craignethan's courtyard walls aesthetically varied, subtle and pleasing, especially when bathed in sunshine.

After writing the sonnet 'To the Walls at Craignethan Castle' I showed it to the guide who asked for a copy; next thing, I was asked by Historic Environment Scotland if they could put it on their Facebook page for National Poetry Day and that is what gave me the idea of writing poems inspired by castle visits.

The castle was built by Sir James Hamilton of Finnart around 1532. Sir James was the Master of Works for James V and was not just a kinsman but a close friend to the King. His fall from grace was sudden, swift, tragic (for him) and not easily explained. One minute he was in favour with the King, but the next he was tried and found guilty of treason (on what may well have been spurious allegations) and executed. He did not get to enjoy his wonderful castle for very long; after his death, ownership passed to the King. 'Confessions of James Hamilton of Finnart' imagines him awaiting execution in the Tolbooth prison in

Edinburgh. I think he may have had cause to feel bitter at the turn of events.

The novel *Old Mortality* by Walter Scott features a castle called Tillietudlem, clearly based on Craignethan, which Scott was known to have visited. In 1856 a station was opened here on the Lesmahagow railway and named Tillietudlem; it was a popular destination for day-trippers visiting the castle in the late 19th and early 20th centuries and inspired the music-hall song 'Tillietudlem Castle'. Eventually, a small village grew here which still bears the name Tillietudlem. 'Reflections on Time and Tillietudlem' could have been written about any or all of the castles I've visited for this project – on the one hand, it is remarkable that they have survived through many centuries, but on the other hand, decay and disintegration seem inevitable, given the forces of time, weather and neglect (not to mention destruction resulting from human conflict).

Craignethan Swallows

On the castle lawn, reclining,
Watching swallows' show-off flight,
Worldly cares are fast receding,
Peaceful as the desert night;
Swallows swooping, entertaining,
Skate on silent blades of light.

Every summer they're arriving
From as far as Timbuktu,
Darting, diving, shifting, twisting,
Stitching quilts of green and blue,
Nearing, veering, disappearing;
Sun and cloud play peek-a-boo.

Insects from the grass are drifting
Lazily into the air,
Dogfight swallows intercepting,
Insects are no longer there,
Baby birds are wide-mouthed, waiting:
Mum and dad will bring their share.

Sadly now we are departing,
Birds and men must go away,
The season's joy will soon be ending
Just as night must follow day;
Halloween is fast approaching
Then the ghosts come out to play.

To the Walls at Craignethan Castle

Honey coloured stones of yellow and brown,
Of buff and beige and cinnamon and straw,
When bathed in sun you soothe away my frown
And make me smile in wonderment and awe.
You take me, dreaming, back to years gone by,
Imagining what stories you might hold –
Of life, of whispered love, of battle cry,
Through hot summer sun or long winter cold.
Your sandstone grit recalls a deeper time
When rocks turned into sand, then sand to stone,
Or so it seems, when on occasion, I'm
Inclined to flights of fancy here alone:
These walls have regular and random forms
As life has both its peacefulness and storms.

Reflections on Time and Tillietudlem

The weakest point? Well, that's the roof,
However strong or well-designed.
We spiderweb those hammer beams
(Think ribcage of a whale);
We engineer the load and lines
And finely fit the joints.
No matter how we wrap it tight
And sweetly seal the seams
Or weld the armadillo scales,
Those lovely interlocking plates
Of solid slabs or slender slates –
It always is the weakest point,
Just look – and see the proof.

That towering, testudo roof
The structure's hat, its crown,
Protects it from all snow and hail
And rain that batters down,
But never is it weather-proof,
In fact it's sure to fail:
Come our neglect or that attack,
The armour gets a chink, a crack
And so it starts,
For entry leads to entropy
As dawning leads to day,
Since ice can fracture stone
And water weakens wood.
Turrets, towers and ramparts,
Crow-step gables, beak-like corbels,
Cornices and crenellations –
All pay the penalty
Of creeping slow decay,

Till we only see foundations
Where something strong once stood.

Don't get me started on chimneys!
I know how much we need a hearth
In this the dampest spot on earth,
But oh, those secret tunnel holes,
Those sneaky downward passageways,
A route for keyhole surgery
By scalpel-wielding elements.
Their stones turn into trolls,
They remind me of Achilles
Or Trojan horse deliveries;
The tiny marching regiments
Of ruin – give me the willies!
And when the roof and floors have gone
Then nature starts to work upon
The stone – and has its way with ease,
On walls like sugar-rotted teeth
And high, stranded fireplaces
(Gaping mouths in monster faces)
With nothing underneath.

This tale of old mortality
Is not one of morality
But just the sheer brutality
Of time – and endless storms and squalls.
The last thing up – the first thing down.
But who, while gazing from these walls
Across the folded land
Could not be pleased that it still stands,
Or ever wish that we had found
A way of building underground?

Confessions of James Hamilton of Finnart

Ah've been ca'd bad names in ma time
An' blamed for wickedness and crimes
By them that would ma clan begrime
And me impugn,
But it's no because o' them that Ah'm
At last brocht doon.

Ah dinna care that Ah've been slandered
Or even ca'd the Arran Bastard,
It isnae lies or names that has stirred
Ma conscience here,
But maybe if ye list ma last words
It will be clear.

In faith, Ah havena aye been good,
Ah hae been gleg in fecht and feud,
Ev'n killed when in an angry mood,
Ah'm sad to say.
Ah ken that nae martyred sainthood
Will come ma way;

But Ah've served the King as well's able,
Abroad and at his board and table,
Proudly managed horse and stable
And by wit and hand
Constructed mony tower and gable
Throughout this land.

Ma finest work at Stirling Palace
Bedazzles like the borealis
And will be praised in songs and ballads
And long adored;
But meanness, devilment and malice
Is ma reward.

Noo James IV was quite a king,
He took me underneath his wing
And gave me boots and shoes and things
When Ah wis wee,
But Flodden was his undoing,
Aye, woe is me!

For efter that we got a bairn,
Too young to talk, too young to reign
And a' the land was under strain
Until he grew –
And then we hoped the whole domain
Would flourish new;

But James was just a twa-faced dandy,
Ower fond o' houghmagandie,
Brawest silks and finest brandy,
Gold and loot;
And as the Gaberlunzie man
He sneaked aboot.

And noo Ah'm in these Tolbooth chains
Suffering anguish, fear and pain
For soon the blood that's in these veins
Will flow like wine;
An' nae doot James's vast domains
Will swallow mine.

One day to James I am a friend
And a' my works he does commend,
The next I am to be condemned
Wi' utmost speed;
To fickleness I owe my end
And kingly greed.

DIRLETON

ONE OF OUR favourite family daytrip destinations, ever since I was a child, has been North Berwick. Dirleton Castle is on the way, so we are certainly no strangers to its charms and it has many; the gardens are wonderfully laid out and maintained, and the bridge leading to the castle gatehouse gives a sense of how it would have been to traverse a real drawbridge over a ditch or moat.

Three noble families inhabited the castle over its 400-year history. Each phase of occupation is reflected in the stone, as successive owners would redesign or rebuild parts of the castle. It is fascinating to look for these architectural clues. It is also interesting to read about the history of the changing fortunes of these families and to imagine what their style and condition of living might have been. These thoughts led to the three sonnets.

East Lothian seems to have been a hotspot for witch trials and persecutions, including the North Berwick witch trials of 1590, a saga which grew out of an alleged plot against the King, and a rash of accusation and trials in 1649 and 1650 in which Dirleton village and castle were involved. 'Burn the Witch' reflects the time when the infamous witch pricker John Kincaid was brought to Dirleton and found the Devil's mark on Patrick Watson and his wife Menie Haliburton. Confessions were never very difficult to extract given the methods they employed and those two, along with five other women, were imprisoned at the castle before being executed on the village green by strangulation and burning.

A number of castles have dovecots, but a particularly well-preserved example is to be found in the grounds of Dirleton Castle. Many pigeons would have been harvested on occasions when a special banquet was planned; given what we know about some of the families who resided at Dirleton, special banquets would probably not have been rare events. I felt a little sorry for the person who had the job of harvesting and preparing pigeons for a feast – hence 'The Pigeon Plucker's Lot'.

Burn the Witch

Burn the witch on the village green,
Burn her man as well,
Burn them baith on the village green
And send them baith tae hell.

There they lie in the castle pit
In the dampness and the dark –
Fetch them here tae the village green
And free them wi' a spark.

Fetch the coals and fetch the tar
Build a dry-wood pyre –
The way tae drive the Devil oot
Is wi' the cleansing fire.

Send the black smoke intae the sky
So's a' the land can tell
The church has fund another witch
And sent her straight tae hell.

Agnes Clarkson soon confessed
And she's already burned –
Peter and Menie she had named
As twa the Deil had turned.

A pricker came to Dirleton,
His name was John Kincaid –
He quickly fund the Devil's mark
That neither hurt nor bled.

The Devil does his wicked wark
Up and doon this land

And he has mony vile recruits
Tae dance at his command.

Ever watchful, ever wary –
We must be on oor guard;
The Devil's hand is everywhere
But we're the hand o' th' Lord.

Burn the witch on the village green,
Burn her man as well,
Burn them baith on the village green
And send them baith tae hell!

The Families of Dirleton Castle

De Vaux

From France they came and settled in this land;
This castle then was built by John de Vaux,
For he was steward to the Scottish Queen,
Who also came from France. From ashlar sand-
Stone blocks he built it, in the French style – so
Elegant and strong; none like it had been
Seen in these parts before: round towers
And a massive curtain wall, on rocky
Outcrop, surrounded by this fertile land:
And so they spent their lordly days and hours
Sleeping, waking, smiling, singing, talking,
The bounty of the country close to hand;
And maybe in their painted rooms, where fires
Burned, red wine from France soothed their hearts' desires.

Haliburton

The Wars of Independence racked this land.
The castle fell (as castles often do)
And then, by marriage, passed into the hands
Of the Haliburtons, who made it new,
Bigger and better, with the grand East Range.
Oh, what a life those Haliburtons knew;
The place baronially rearranged
Held luxury and comfort through and through.

Those well-stocked cellars underneath the Hall
Supplied the wares for banquet, feast and ball;
The massive kitchen's lively, bustling scene
Thrumming like a well-maintained machine
And from their lofty tower in times of calm,
That view, of Craigleith, Fidra and the Lamb.

Ruthven

The castle passed by marriage once again;
The Ruthven Lords were next to run the place –
They seemed to favour courtly plots and schemes
(One was involved when Rizzio was slain)
But then they flew too high and fell from grace
And paid the price for those ambitious dreams.
They built this Ruthven Lodging and for years
They filled its rooms with children and with noise
(There may yet be an echo in the stone),
But laughter soon gave way to bitter tears
And sad regrets were commoner than joys,
When Lady Dorothea lived alone,
Reflecting on their downfall and their shame
And how they lost their status and their name.

The Pigeon Plucker's Lot

Feathers and blood and shit,
That's my daily chore;
In misery I sit
And pluck a hundred doves,
Sometimes even more.
I wish they'd give me gloves
(My fingers get so sore);
They don't think of that –
It might make plucking slower.
So I sit here like a twat,
Such a plucking bore,
Feathers all around me,
Suffering the stink
Of excrement and gore
From the pigeons that surround me –
Half the bloody doocot.
I'd rather stir the stewpot,
I'd rather sweep the floor,
I'd even turn the spit –
Though the fire gets so hot –
I'd rather sit and knit,
Instead I curse my lot:
This greasy crop-bag grit;
Feathers and blood and shit!

DOUNE

DOUNE CASTLE WAS built in the late 1300s by Robert Stewart, 1st Duke of Albany, Earl of Menteith and Fife. Albany, one of the sons of Robert II, is sometimes remembered as 'Scotland's uncrowned king'. He acted as High Chamberlain of Scotland from 1382 and later as Regent until his death in 1420. Certainly, Doune Castle, in its heyday, would have been impressive enough to rank with the royal castles of the period.

Doune Castle is still impressive, perhaps because it never suffered serious damage in siege or attack and was restored in Victorian times, and so most of the roof remains intact. Situated close to the main route from Edinburgh and Stirling to the Highlands, it is a castle that I have visited frequently.

Doune is yet another castle that has been used as a filming location, most famously for *Monty Python and the Holy Grail*, parts of which were filmed here in 1974. My favourite part of the film is where John Cleese employs his 'outrageous [French] accent' to taunt and berate Arthur and his Knights of the Round Table from the battlements. The conclusion to the comedic exchange comes when Cleese decides it is time for action rather than words and gives the order '*Fetchez la vache!*' A cow is then catapulted over the walls to land among the Arthurian entourage.

As a folk singer, I was long aware of the traditional song 'The Bonnie Earl o' Moray' and its connection to Doune Castle. It is a sad and romantic ballad about the death of the famously good-looking James Stewart, 2nd Lord Doune and 2nd Earl of Moray. In 1581 he married Elizabeth Stewart who was the eldest daughter of Regent Moray (also called James Stewart, confusingly). It was through this marriage that the Bonnie Earl acquired his title.

Unhappily for him, he got into a feud with George Gordon, 6th Earl of Huntly (later the 1st Marquis). Huntly was given permission by King James VI to arrest Moray, who had been accused of treason, and to bring him to trial. Huntly cornered Moray at his home in Donibristle in Fife and set fire to the house. Moray managed to escape the burning building but was pursued to the rocky shore and murdered by Huntly. This was definitely overstepping his brief in order to settle personal scores, but the King seems to have turned a blind eye.

Elizabeth, his wife (or 'his lady' in the song), apparently died in childbirth in 1591 and the Donibristle events by all accounts took place on 7 February 1592, so it seems she could not have been looking 'o'er frae castle Doune' for her husband's return as she was already dead. However, a painting commissioned by the Earl's mother, showing the wounds on his dead body, bears the inscription '1591 Febr. 7', so there is a bit of confusion.

It is not that I have any fascination for latrine closets, but they do at least remind me how lucky we are these days to have centrally heated bathrooms with hot running water and flushing toilets. Latrine chutes must, on occasion, have been places where chilly updrafts would make lingering unpleasant and the form of waste disposal was pretty primitive.

Thoughts like these were in my head when I looked up from the courtyard at Doune Castle and was able to see into a latrine chute at the top of the kitchen tower. I figured out that this latrine provided a toilet outflow for the room which is described in the guidebook as 'Mary Queen of Scots' Bedchamber' because she spent the night in that very room on 13 September 1563 – and so the inspiration for 'The Queen's Bahookie' seemed to just fall from the sky.

Fetchez la Vache!

Mon Dieu; sacré bleu!
Is it true? *Oui, c'est vrai —*
Ils parlent Français;
Le château de Doune
By foreign buffoons
Appears to be now *occupé*.

But here comes Arthur on coconut steed,
A king on a quest after valiant deeds;
He's seeking the Grail, the holy cup,
And he wants them to lift the drawbridge up
So he starts with the French to *parler*.

But the French are so rude
(*C'est leur habitude*)
Not quite *élan vital*,
More like *un petit mal*,
And they don't want
Entente cordiale.
By their helmets and mittens
They don't like the Britons
(*On ne sait pas pourquoi*)
Especially Arthur, *le Roi*.

The one on the battlements
Blows raspberry flatulence,
Cursing the knights down below;
'In your direction I fart,
You think you are smart –
If you are you'll depart;
We don't give a damn, Sir,
Your mum was a hamster
And your dad smelt of elderberries.'

He sneers from the parapet,
This is no *tête-à-tête*,
This Frenchman's totally hyper,
'Go boil your bottoms
With your soiled cottons
You animal food-trough wiper';
If Arthur was a fly, he would swat him.

Then, quick as a flash
And with lordly *panache*
He barks out the order,
'Fetchez la vache!'

Then straight away
Une vache jetée
Était tiré
D'un trébuchet.
And over the walls
The flying cow soars;
It revolves
And it falls
On the English knights
And beefily smites
One full sore.

So the Britons retreat
From this high-flying cow
And various other *oiseaux et bêtes*,
For they know they are beat,
Leastways for now.
To get a result
And to win *le château*
They may have to consult
Chrétien de Troyes –
Now he is the boy,

In Arthurian lore,
He knows the score
For he is no fool
And maybe he'll pull
Un lapin de son chapeau.

The Bonnie Earl o' Moray

'Oh lang may his lady
Look o'er frae Castle Doune
Ere she see the Earl o' Moray
Come soundin' thru' the toon.'

Another ambitious young man,
An aristocrat on the make,
A story of schemes and of plans,
Of blunders, designs and mistakes,
Of chessboards and pulling of strings
And the fears of a paranoid king.

Though Moray was comely and fair,
The young Earl was out of his league;
He fell into Earl Huntly's snare
(That master of wiles and intrigue)
And there on the dark shore of Fife
Earl Moray was robbed of his life.

Now this was a dastardly deed
And some thought the killer should die,
But Huntly fled northwards with speed
And James chose to turn a blind eye;
Much later this unpunished wrong
Was captured in popular song.

We sing of a grief-stricken dame,
Elizabeth, all in a swoon;
The bonny Earl no' comin' hame,
She stares from the castle at Doune;
But by songs we are sometimes misled
For that lady was already dead.

The Queen's Bahookie

Ah'm jist a mislernit minker
An' she is o' highest degree,
But Ah saw the royal bahookie
When the Queen wis ha'ein' a pee.

Ah wis oot in the yaird o' the castle
Tidyin' roond and aboot,
The sky wis blue as a robin's egg –
'Twas a fine day – there's nae dispute.

Ah didnae expect tae get rained oan,
But suddenly Ah heard a splash,
So Ah lookit up towards the roof
An' jist got a wee, fleetin' flash.

A bare, white bahookie, lookin' at me,
Doon frae that lofty latrine;
Ah remembered who wis ludgin' up there
Ower the kitchen – the Queen!

Ah scampered awa' in a hurry,
But no tae avoid the wee;
Ah kent if Ah wis seen keekin' at that
It micht be hot water for me.

The next few days Ah skulked aboot
An' must hiv seemed quite withdrawn;
Ah couldnae get oot o' ma mind the behind
That Ah had been gazin' upon.

An' Ah've often thocht since
If she'd looked at me yince
Ma face wad be bleezin,
Ah'd be guilty o' treason
An' baith legs wad end up in splints.

But Ah guess Ah've escaped retribution,
Though really Ah wisnae tae blame;
Nae cause tae feel shame
So Ah claim absolution
For castin' ma een
Oan a part o' the Queen
That Ah really never should name.

Ah'm jist a mislernit minker
An' she is o' highest degree,
But Ah saw the royal bahookie
When the Queen wis ha'ein' a pee.

DUNDONALD

ON MY FIRST visit to Dundonald, I discovered a castle that seems to epitomise the idea of a story told in stone. The present extent of Dundonald is a reasonably intact ruin of a castle built by Robert II in the 14th century to replace a larger castle built by Alexander, the High Steward in the late 13th century (which was probably destroyed by Robert the Bruce); this castle in turn replaced a motte and bailey edifice constructed more than a hundred years before – and there is evidence of a hill fort preceding that.

Of course, Dundonald has also been altered and added to over the years, and significant parts of the structure are now missing. It is a puzzle in many ways: how was the prison pit accessed? Why were there two halls? Where were the bedchambers? (Robert II had 21 children, so this really is curious.) The castle contains fascinating traces of carved faces and animals, and many other interesting features and mysteries in masonry. Like most castles, it is not difficult to look at the great hall, the minstrels' gallery or the prison pit and to imagine sounds, sights and smells that reverberate down the years from the little hammerings of humanity on the adamantine anvil of time.

My first poem, 'Approaching Dundonald', was inspired by the stunning view of the castle on that bright morning when I first saw it, with the Saltire fluttering above the battlements and a still clearly visible full moon slipping towards the horizon.

On that visit, I was accompanied by my ten-year-old daughter and one of her friends. The trip down the ladder into the prison pit was an adventure for them, especially when they realised the place had become a home for a large number of impressive spiders. This gave me a chance to write about a prison dungeon from a slightly unusual angle – and to have a bit of fun with 'Dundonald Prison Pit'.

My villanelle with the title 'The Dundonald Ring' demonstrates the importance of talking to castle guides whenever possible. They are great sources of history's facts and fables, and many of them have an obvious interest in and affection for the sites that they work in. On this occasion, the guide I spoke to told me that another guide had found a ring on a molehill in the grounds of the castle. The ring had been sent to Historic Environment Scotland and was being studied. It seems it was probably mediaeval and bore the images of a thistle and a rose. If I hadn't been chatting to the guide, I would never have learned about this useful little nugget.

Approaching Dundonald

The castle stood in clear relief
Against a cobalt sky;
Above its walls the tardy moon
Was like a Cyclops eye

That slowly moved towards the ground
As if seduced by sleep,
Or caught beyond the curfew hour
And so did guilty creep;

But also there, above the walls,
A saltire surfed the breeze
And waved farewell to the shifty moon
As gallous as you please;

So now the thing that sticks with me
Like memorising glue –
Dundonald ramparts were the mount
For a study of white on blue.

Dundonald Prison Pit

I found myself in the prison pit
At Dundonald for my crimes.
I quickly ran out of things to do
To help me pass the time,
Until I saw in the constant gloom
That I was not alone;
A hundred spiders all around
Watching me from the stone.

I gave them names to amuse myself,
They treat me like their chum:
Peter Parker, Sigourney Weaver,
Zorro and Speidi Klum;
There's one called Arnold Schwarzenlegger,
He's big and dumb and thick,
There's Furry Boots frae Aberdeen,
Miss Muffet, Barb and Nick.

Some of the spiders sing me songs
To give my heart a lift,
There's Jimmy Webb and the Spinners too,
And Tarantaylor Swift;
There's Sting and one whose voice is deep
Though his movements are quite jaunty,
A bit like dancing the tarantella
With Hairy Bellyfonte.

There's Attercop and Aragog
And one that's called Shelob;
Jenny, Charlotte and Legolas too,
Peek-a-boo and Bob.
There's Frankenspider and William Hare,

They scare me when they jump,
There's one high up above the rest:
I call her Arania Trump.

Of course, there's one that I call Bruce,
Not just cos he's the boss,
But he makes me think that I might find
That not all hope is lost.
There's Incy Wincy, Venom and Fang,
Each has their place on the wall
And one that I call Michael Phelps:
He's good at doing the crawl.

Some are nice like Tickle and Fluff,
But others make me wish
I could give them nasty little names
Like Flushed or Splat or Squish;
But I'd never want to harm them,
I only show them love;
They cannot hurt me, after all,
And they're all the friends I have.

The Dundonald Ring

A ring appeared from underneath the clay,
A mole had brought it up from underground;
The past is never very far away.

A tour guide saw it catch the light one day
And he could not believe what he had found;
A ring appeared from underneath the clay.

It's nice that fortune still has tricks to play,
The tether of the earth can be unbound;
The past is never very far away.

Our minds race back through countless yesterdays,
Two thousand seasons may have spun around
Till a ring appeared from underneath the clay;

We wonder how it might have gone astray,
By treachery, by theft, on battleground?
The past is never very far away.

Perhaps in truth it simply was mislaid,
Though much more artful theories will abound,
How rings appear from underneath the clay.

Our artefacts live on though we decay.
What's gone can be both buried and profound,
But when rings appear from underneath the clay
The past is never very far away.

DUNSTAFFNAGE

MY VISIT TO Dunstaffnage was a family road trip through stunning scenery to a very special location, so well worth the time and effort. I couldn't persuade the family to take in Oban distillery afterwards, but the seafood hut on the pier was just as enjoyable.

Dunstaffnage's location is not only beautiful but also of strategic importance – at least it would have been in the early centuries of its existence. It sits on a promontory in the Firth of Lorn which both gives it protection and commands the seaways in that part of Argyll. This was particularly important in the 13th century, when the whole area was a frontier between the Lords of the Isles and the kingdom of Scotland.

Dunstaffnage was built in 1220 by Duncan MacDougall, a grandson of Somerled (the first King of the Isles), and it was a MacDougall stronghold until the Wars of Independence, when the MacDougalls decided to support John Balliol and found they had backed the wrong horse. Robert the Bruce defeated them in battle at the Pass of Brander, sent them packing to England and seized Dunstaffnage.

For over 150 years the castle was owned by the Crown, looked after by a succession of keepers. In 1463, the keeper, John Stewart of Lorn, while on his way to be married, was murdered by Alan MacDougall (some of the clan appear to have sneaked back from England). MacDougall seized the castle and took up unlawful residence. However, King James III sent troops to oust him and the castle was given over to Colin Campbell, 1st Earl of Argyll. The annual rental to be paid by the Campbells was set at 'a plaid, a red rose, a pair of gloves and two silver pennies'. This was the story behind the sonnet 'Colin Campbell comes to Dunstaffnage'.

The second sonnet, 'A Captain's Life', was not written about any keeper or captain in particular, but is just a reflection on some aspects of that role and how it might have felt to carry the duties and responsibilities of looking after the castle and keeping the peace in that part of Scotland – and what some of the compensations might have been.

Finally, the villanelle picks up a moment in the castle's history during the Jacobite Rebellion. The

Campbells were on the side of the Crown and after the defeat of Bonnie Prince Charlie there were many reprisals against supporters of the Young Pretender. In 1746 Flora MacDonald, who had helped Charlie to escape, was arrested and held prisoner at Dunstaffnage before being sent to the Tower of London. She was actually released the following year, but she could easily have been tried and executed for treason and her mind must have been full of the fear of this possibility while she was pacing the floor at Dunstaffnage.

Colin Campbell Comes to Dunstaffnage

My name is Colin Campbell of Argyll,
Dunstaffnage is the place I now reside;
I think that I can live here in some style
And keep the peace throughout the countryside.
MacDougall squatted here without the right,
But James was not content for him to stay;
He quit the place in shame without a fight,
James kicked him out and sent him on his way.
He then chose me to take the castle on,
To occupy and keep in good repair
And I will do my best to honour him
As long as this fine keep is in my care.
The yearly rent – a pair of gloves, a shawl,
Two silver pennies and a rose – that's all.

A Captain's Life

As captain of this castle I control
The land routes and the sea ways of the west.
On good days it's a diplomatic role,
Though sometimes strength of arms is put to test.
The politics of kings and clans are such
That keep me pretty lively on my toes,
My chance of relaxation is not much
With entertaining guests and chasing foes.
The sheltered bay nearby is such a gift
And sometimes boats arrive from far-off lands;
The wines and spices give our days a lift –
It feels like we hold sunlight in our hands.
On winter nights some sunshine in a glass
Can help to make the hours of darkness pass.

Flora MacDonald Fears for her Future

I cannot bear to live and not be free,
I pace the floor from morning until night;
But I can hear the birds and smell the sea.

I'm here because I helped the prince to flee.
I felt for him and saw his desp'rate plight,
For I can't bear to live and not be free.

I wish that in my hand I held the key
Or somehow found the magic pow'r of flight,
For I can hear the birds and smell the sea.

And now they say transported I must be
And locked up in the Tow'r of London tight;
I cannot bear to live and not be free,

And what the future holds I can't foresee;
Some things are maybe better out of sight,
But yet I hear the birds and smell the sea.

Soon these small comforts will be lost to me;
I stand accused as traitor Jacobite.
I cannot bear to live and not be free
While yet I hear the birds and smell the sea.

EDINBURGH

EDINBURGH IS MY hometown, so I grew up under the ever-present shadow of Edinburgh Castle, a magnificent crowning edifice on a dominating natural feature, 'the rock'.

At school we heard stories of attackers climbing the castle rock by night; we learned about ancient volcanoes and how glaciers encountered the rock and shaped the backbone of the old town and most years we attended the Military Tattoo. As a teenager, I worked (and lived) in the Palace Hotel as a kitchen porter and my bedroom window looked out from the lofty hotel rooftop across to the castle. When my children were young, we regularly enjoyed the Festival fireworks concert when the castle's silhouette became even more dramatic than usual, and during the '80s and early '90s I sang folksongs in the Ensign Ewart, a pub named after a famous soldier whose memorial stands close by on the castle esplanade.

Finding poetic inspiration for this castle, therefore, was not too difficult. The first sonnet pays tribute to the ancient volcanic plug of 'This Castle Rock', mentions St Margaret's Chapel (the building which fascinated me most as I gazed across from my bedroom window in the Palace Hotel, Castle Street) and reminds us of the various military roles and features of the castle.

The second sonnet describes a tale from the *Y Gododdin*, a mediaeval poem in which we find the first recorded mention of Edinburgh Castle. It could be a scene from an action movie – but you have to wonder why anyone thought that a year of feasting and drinking mead was a suitable preparation for battle.

The third sonnet is about Cannonball House. I have taken many visitors around Edinburgh Castle, where I can proudly show off the beauty of my hometown, and I always point out the cannonball lodged in the wall of this building. There are doubters of course, but why would anyone want to undermine a good story?

'The Black Dinner' recounts one of the more gruesome stories from the castle's history; in 1440 the 16-year-old William Douglas, 6th Earl of Douglas and his younger brother David were invited to dine at the castle with the ten-year-old

King James II. During the dinner a black bull's head (a symbol of death) was placed on the table and, despite the protests of the young King, the Douglas brothers were immediately dragged outside and executed.

One of the 'noblemen' involved in this plot was James Douglas, great uncle to the boys; their death meant that he became the 7th Earl. Incidentally, James Douglas died about three years later and was succeeded by his son William (who would have been about the same age as the William who was executed). In 1452, this William, the 8th Earl, was invited to Stirling Castle by the now adult James II. Following an argument, William was stabbed in the throat by the King; the Captain of the Guard 'struck out his brains with a pole ax', in the words of *The Auchinleck Chronicle*, and then his body was thrown out of the window. What goes around comes around.

This Castle Rock

Thrown up from the mantle's molten magma
And hardened into adamantine stone;
Ice sheets and erosion-carved enigmas
Of landscapes that once were, but now are gone.
Centuries have swept St Margaret's Chapel
(Attacks and clash of arms and bloody war)
And yet this oldest building in the castle
Can turn our war to peace behind its door.
But so we are not fooled by this illusion,
Every day at one a gun goes off;
See regimental records in profusion
And vast displays of military stuff –
Too much for some, but all these signs and shrines
Preserve the castle's purpose in our minds.

First Recorded Mention of Edinburgh Castle

An old Brittonic poem tells the tale
Of how the chieftain of the tribe Gododdin
Had gathered round him heroes hard and hale,
An army, to the fortress of Din Eidyn.
They were the pick of battle-hardened men,
With steady eyes, cool heads and sturdy grip;
Their polished weapons glittered in the sun,
With whetted blades and balanced shafts, keen-tipped.
They lived there for a year upon the rock
With mead and feasting almost every night
Until they were unleashed and ran amok,
Berserk on mead and eager for the fight.
On Catt'rick then they surged upon their foes,
But mead-befuddled, fell, like dominoes.

Cannonball House

This castle has been often under siege –
When Grange held out for Mary Queen of Scots,
Or later on, when Covenanters seized
And held it, or when Jacobites fired shots.
Now each of these assaults came from the town
And every time the garrison replied
With cannon fire that knocked whole buildings down
(They knew they could be killed if forced outside).
And so this house, right in the line of fire,
Has a ball in the wall – that story rings
Quite true; but there are some who call me 'liar' –
'It's just the water level from the Springs
At Comiston'. Some dullards never fail
To pour cold water on a gripping tale.

The Black Dinner

The table shook.
The children jumped
With fear, alarm and shock,
Wire-taut, their hearts and brains;
William, David and the young King James.

A grisly thing had just been dumped
Upon the board,
Scattering knives and plates;
The severed head
Of a bovine beast.
Terror unleashed,
Their instincts were to run
From this grotesque and gruesome game;

The massive, bulging eyes
That stared,
The flopping tongue,
Hard horn, soft ears,
Nostrils oozing drops of blood
And even more blood dripping
From that outrageous, disconnected neck
And all those thick black hairs.

They turn their gaze
From that now muted maw
To the men that stood around
And all they saw
Was one unmoving crowd
With one grim face.

THE QUEEN'S BAHOOKIE

Before they could make sense
Of these events,
David and William were seized
And roughly taken
Out to Castlehill in black of night.
Words were harshly spoken
And trust and truth and chivalry
Were broken.

Lies and truth, truth and lies
Swirling round like wind-tossed leaves
Were swept across the cobbles and away.
Their wretched cries
Echoed off embarrassed, silent stones
And a stoic silver moon shone
Down through cold November skies.

From somewhere
There appeared an axe,
A dark and heavy block;
Then two swift strokes
And the black bull's head back there
Had small but noble company.

ELCHO

ELCHO CASTLE IS a brilliant piece of architecture; as you walk around the building it displays a continually changing face of towers, turrets, roofscapes and features, in much the way that a fantastical place like Gormenghast might have done.

It was built around 1560 by the Wemyss family and, not unusually for 16th-century castles, although it has the appearance of a defensive structure, it was intended more as an impressive mansion or country house – a family seat in the castle style. Impressive it certainly is, both inside and out, and with its gardens and orchards and its position by the shores of the Tay, it would have been a wonderful lodging for an important family.

In the hall I saw two magnificent candelabras; although these were gifted to Elcho in 2002, they give a hint of the opulence that might have been on display here around 1600 when the castle was in its heyday. Candelabras like this would have been important in the days before oil lamps and electricity. Each one supports nine candles and seeing these wonderful artefacts inspired the reverie of 'My Candelabras'.

In a similar vein, the time I spent in the kitchen and larder made me think about some of the skills that would have been necessary for turning the local produce into meals and entertainment for a large number of people, long before gas or electric ovens and hobs. Everything would have been cooked or smoked in the massive fireplace. We get some idea of this from illustrations in various castles of the use of roasting spits (controlled by the turnbrochie), the skilfully layered cauldrons and the baking and brewing processes that must have been happening continually on an almost industrial scale. There would have also been huge effort put into preserving, pickling, salting and smoking produce for the winter months. My poem 'King of Fish' describes how the cook might have received a salmon from the Tay and smoked it in the chimney.

The 'Song of the Woodcutter' is about one of the unsung heroes of the castle era. I imagine that an important job in a castle of this size was to keep it supplied with fuel for the many chamber fireplaces, the kitchen, the bakehouse and the alehouse – not an easy job. If this woodcutter did his job well, there would always be warmth, comfort and cheer in the castle, though I doubt if he ever got the praise he deserved. On the other hand, he surely would have been cursed if the fuel ran out or was too damp to burn well in the depths of a Scottish winter.

My Candelabras

I had these candelabras made
By blacksmiths in the town;
I love the flickering light and shade
Of candle flames that leap and play
And flutter, gutter, swing and sway
Upon the walls around.

On winter nights when hard winds blow
And shake the castle slates,
My candelabras gleam and glow
And cast a magic shadow show
That seems to make the time pass slow
And winter storms abate.

Within the fire the seasoned wood
Throws heat into the hall,
It warms us through and cooks our food
And every day must be renewed,
But candlelight is clean and good
And that's the best of all.

When everyone's asleep in bed
I sit here late at night,
A glass of wine, a piece of bread,
With happy thoughts inside my head;
I should be sleeping but instead
I watch the dancing light.

A single candle shines at night,
Some pilgrim left behind;
In church small candles flicker bright,
But eighteen candles are a sight,
A sacred symphony of light
To please all humankind.

King of Fish

A fisherman came calling here this morning
With the King of Fish he'd wrestled from the Tay;
I laid my acquisition
On a table in the kitchen
And the fisherman went whistling with his pay.

I washed it clean; I gutted it and skinned it,
Then neatly cut each side from off the bone;
Then to make it nice and scrummy
I rubbed in salt and honey
And a few dried herbs – the recipe's my own.

Then I fetched the blackened board with v-cut edges
And I tied the pieces on it, side by side,
And I left it there to pickle
While its juices slowly trickled
And by eventide the fish was nicely dried.

When the bustle of the evening meal was over
I smoored the glowing embers down with ash,
Then I hoisted up the chimney,
In a corner lit but dimly,
That board to which the salmon now was lashed.

Then, carefully, I spread across the embers
Some chips of applewood that had been soaked
And I left the fish suspended,
Completely unattended,
To draw some flavour from the rolling smoke.

ELCHO

I know that when Lord Elcho comes to breakfast
And he sees that fine smoked salmon on its dish,
His weary eye will brighten
And his countenance will lighten
For he always loves a bit of well-smoked fish.

That royal fish once battled up the river
Against the water's flow, so sleek and spry;
Its struggle now is ended;
It was epic, it was splendid,
But smoke now curls and swims towards the sky.

Song of the Woodcutter

I

That steward struts about the place,
A haughty look upon his face;
He treats all others with disdain,
This buttery and pantry thane.
He jangles keys and holds his purse
To reign the castle universe.

The cook wins constant nods of praise,
Especially on holidays
When feasts and banquets are prepared
For dignitaries and the Laird.

The baker thinks we'd all drop dead
Except she makes our daily bread;
The alewife thinks the Holy Grail
Is not too good to hold her ale.

It's true they have a part to play,
They're all important in their way
And I do not hold strong desire
To be admired for making fire,
But without me, if truth were told,
They all might perish from the cold
And who could bake or brew or cook
Without the fire in ingle nook.

II

For I am the wayward woodcutting man,
I comb these woods and dells
And I tramp the tracks of the woodland realm
Of beech and oak, of ash and elm,
From the dark wood's heart to the gorse bush edge;
Like rabbit runs through a brambly hedge
These paths I know so well.

Yes, I am the wayward woodcutting man,
I watch for fallen boughs,
I coppice and cut and pollard and prune,
Like the woodland birds I whistle my tune
And as many branches and logs are stacked
Or carried by cart up the woodland track
As the weather and time allows.

The skin of this wayward woodcutting man
In summer is chestnut brown;
My arms are strong from wielding the axe,
My hands have calluses, blisters and hacks,
But for all the hard work I never complain
For the warm smiling sun and the soft healing rain
Are better than wearing a crown.

The skill of the wayward woodcutting man
Is knowing the woodland lore;
Which logs will burn with a heart-lifting scent
And which ones will smoke or spark to torment;
It's knowing the weather and planning ahead,
It's stocking the cords and filling the shed
And never depleting the store.

So think of the wayward woodcutting man
When nights are dismal and dank,
When your fire lights at the taper's touch,
When a dying fire is revived by brush,
When your guests are jolly and loosening their ties
And the firelight gleams in your children's eyes,
For I am the fellow to thank.

HAILES

HAILES CASTLE WAS built by the de Gourlay family (originally from Northumberland) sometime in the 13th century. Parts of the castle are therefore very old and it stands on a rocky outcrop looking over the river Tyne, not far from East Linton. The location, these days, is somewhat off the beaten track and it is perhaps the only castle I visited for this project which does not have a visitor centre, being open to the public without charge.

During the Wars of Independence, the de Gourlays sided with the English and supported John Balliol, so when he lost in the contest to gain the Scottish crown, they lost control of the castle, which then came under the care of the Earl of Dunbar. In the 14th century it was acquired by the Hepburn family and legend has it that Adam Hepburn was given the castle as a reward for saving the Earl of Dunbar from an attack by a savage horse. That story lies behind the first poem.

The second poem, written in ballad form, describes another episode from the castle's history, this time the more verifiable story of an attack on the castle by Henry 'Hotspur' Percy in the year 1400. This siege was unsuccessful and Henry Percy was chased back to Alnwick in a counter attack by Archibald, Master of Douglas (soon to become the 4th Earl of Douglas on the death of his father, Archibald the Grim). There were many skirmishes between the English and the Scots around this time, and it seems that the nickname 'Hotspur' was applied to Henry Percy by the Scots because of his readiness to take up arms and attack them at any opportunity.

I visited Hailes on a wet day in November and the final poem, 'Address to the Old Hailes Burn', was a kind of promise to come back and see the place in a different season, for I know that the experience of visiting these castles can be entirely different depending on the time of year, the weather and other factors. The poem's form is a nod to Tennyson's poem 'The Brook'.

|

The Savage Horse

Across this pimpled, sea-fringed borderland
My mind's eye rose and soared – just like a hawk
That hovers, watching ev'ry bush and rock,
When something caught my eye upon the strand;
'Twas no beached whale, no cart couped in a ditch,
Nor yet the smoke from some poor burning witch;

But in a paddock there, I saw a horse,
Black as the shadow cast by hell's back door,
It neighed like a screech from a foundry floor
And answered not to kindness or to force.
With anvil-heavy hoof it pawed the ground,
Its temper shook the countryside around;

And trapped inside that paddock was the Earl,
A man not used to ever giving way,
A man whose strong authority held sway
O'er all the tenants of his Dunbar world,
But suddenly the fury was unleashed
Upon him of this coal-black, savage beast.

Entranced, I watched the dreadful scene unfold,
My fancy flying far beyond the clouds;
The Earl, a man so haughty and so proud,
No longer acting quite so brash and bold,
But trembling, panicked, fearful and dismayed
He glanced to left and right in hope of aid.

Just then, across the fence, young Hepburn leapt,
A hero from some old, fantastic tale.
The horse reared up and made its front hooves flail

But he between the brute and Dunbar stepped;
He cast his cape across the horse's head
And Dunbar seized his chance and quickly fled.

But Hepburn did not flee – he stood his ground
And whether it was rash, or wise,
He started singing out – his tenor voice
Was loud and clear: this unexpected sound
The horse did seem to quiet and confuse
And stilled the terror in its thrashing hooves.

And as he softer made the song he sang,
That steed by steps and stages calmer grew,
Until it seemed to settle and to know
That it had heard the true horse whispering;
And now those storm clouds seemed to disappear
And ocean's roar no longer vexed the ear.

Now who can say what made that horse go wild?
A poisoned herb or wicked witch's spell?
Some creatures are just born savage, and ill
Temper their default state. The Devil's child
Is not an easy thing to bring to peace
But Hepburn was the man to calm this beast.

The truth behind this tale we'll never know,
But what we do know is the Earl was safe
And grateful to his saviour for his life.
He was a man with riches to bestow,
So Hepburn won Hailes Castle – and of course
He also got to keep the savage horse.

Hotspur Hastened Hotfoot Home

Henry Percy crossed the border
With his band of knights;
The Scots had nicknamed Percy 'Hotspur' –
Always keen to fight.

On they came, their spears a-glist'ning
Over hill and dell,
Up from Alnwick they came whistling,
Bent on raising hell.

Once again the Tweed was forded,
England left behind;
Scottish settlements unguarded
Lost their peace of mind.

Deep into the Scottish heartland
Percy led his men,
Villages attacked and scarred and
Burnt to ash again.

Near East Linton these invaders
Set their camp and then
On to Hailes the warlike raiders
Challenged its defence.

Twice they cast their might upon it,
Both times were repelled,
Ranted round it histrionic,
Damning all to Hell.

Off to camp once more at sunset,
There to plan a siege,

There to think what might be done yet
To bring it to its knees.

Through that long, cold, winter darkness
Hotspur drank his wine,
Fumed and cursed and howled his madness
Across the River Tyne.

Just two hours before the dawning,
Douglas broke their peace;
Charged the camp and gave no warning,
Smote them down like fleas.

Suddenly, the tables turning,
Attackers now attacked,
Their camp in ruins, chattels burning,
Demons at their back.

Hotspur hotfoot back to Alnwick
Fast as he could fly,
English knights and men in panic,
Many soon would die.

Master Douglas reached the border,
Hero of the fight,
All his men in perfect order
Back to Hailes that night.

Tyne flows peaceful, soft, unhurried,
By Hailes castle walls;
Once again the rats have scurried
Back into their holes.

Address to Old Hailes Burn

November days are short and dank,
Today it's grey and cloudy;
I see you've risen up your banks
And now run by me loudly.

The trees have given up their leaves,
Your courses clogged and cluttered,
Towards the Tyne you rush with ease
Your water chocolate coloured.

Some other day I may return
To find a bright sun shining,
Blue sky reflected in the burn
And picnic folk reclining.

In summertime when days are dry
You barely show a trickle,
But feathered friends sing in your sky,
By thistle heads you're tickled.

Beneath a silver winter moon
I hear your icy chatter,
By frozen fronds of grass festooned
As snowflakes slowly scatter.

Around this castle on you flow
In every kind of weather
And men may come and men may go
But you go on forever.

HUNTINGTOWER

THIS CASTLE WAS built by the Ruthven family, probably around 1500. It seems to have consisted of two almost side-by-side towers right from the start, though part of the stonework in the lower part of the east tower may pre-date this. The enigma of why two towers were constructed in close proximity is addressed in the first poem, 'Twin Towers'.

Despite this seemingly odd construction, in its heyday Huntingtower would have been a very impressive set of buildings, including a great hall and other extensions long since demolished.

The castle was originally known as The Place of Ruthven and the Ruthven family were of high standing in Scotland, having been appointed Sheriffs of Perth by Robert the Bruce in reward for their service and allegiance during the Wars of Independence. The story behind the second poem 'The Ruthven Raid' is jam-packed with almost incredible snippets of power struggles and courtly intrigue. In August 1582, William Ruthven, Treasurer of Scotland, 4th Lord Ruthven and 1st Earl of Gowrie, basically imprisoned the 16-year-old King James VI in this castle. The King managed to escape ten months later, and though he initially pardoned William Ruthven, something else happened the following year (more plotting perhaps?), which made him change his mind; Ruthven was then arrested, tried and executed.

Two years after this, James VI restored the estates and titles to William's son James, who died soon after and was succeeded in 1588 by John Ruthven, apparently quite the Renaissance man. In 1600, it seems that John Ruthven lured the King to his house in Perth and tried to lock him in. The King was rescued and his would-be captor and his brother, Alexander, were killed. James VI was so annoyed by this second attempt to detain or abduct him that the corpses of John and Alexander were put on trial in Edinburgh, found guilty of treason and then publicly hung, drawn and quartered. The name of Ruthven was abolished and the castle was renamed Huntingtower.

A somewhat more private and domestic intrigue inspired the third poem, 'The Maiden's Leap'. William,

4th Lord Ruthven, and his wife, Janet, had 14 children and one of them, Dorothea, was in love with John Wemyss of Pittencrieff. The legend of The Maiden's Leap refers to this courtship, which was apparently not approved by Dorothea's parents. While Wemyss was visiting the castle, they were careful to accommodate him in the tower that did not include Dorothea's chamber. Nevertheless, she managed to get into his room and to avoid being discovered when her suspicious mother was banging on the door, she leapt in the dark from the roof of one tower to the next, a gap of 2.7 metres. The lovers seem to have evaded detection on this occasion, but they decided to elope and get married the very next day.

Twin Towers

Why would you ever build two towers
So close up, side by side?

Given the amount of stone involved,
You don't gain space inside

And think of all the extra stairs
To keep servants occupied.

Was the builder seeing double
When he read the plan?

Was it a family divided?
Was the son a difficult man?

Or was there a husband and a wife
Who never could agree?

Maybe the husband snored a lot
And she wanted to be free.

Perhaps it's just aesthetics,
Though symmetry's not displayed –

The towers are slightly unaligned
And the roofs face different ways.

We'll never know the reason
For this almost balancing act,

But as we've learned in later years
Twin towers need two attacks.

The Ruthven Raid

Dinnae mess wi' James the sixth
If ye want tae keep yer heid;
William Ruthven locked him up,
Noo Lord William's deid.

He locked up James for near a year,
A rather curious thing –
Did naeb'dy bother tae enquire
Whit happened tae the King?

Efter ten month locked away,
He managed tae get oot
By makin' wings o' pigeon feathers
Or bribin' a maid wi' loot.

Yince oot an' free, ye'd think the King
Wad need nae ither reason,
But it took a year afore Lord Ruthven
Stood trial for High Treason.

Noo back in those days justice wis
Whatever the King decreed,
So the executioner dealt the chop –
Lopped aff his heid wi' speed.

The Ruthven tribe were dispossessed
And lost their family hame;
Cast tae the wilderness (east o' Dundee)
Mired in grief and shame.

But no much longer eftir that
The King had a change o' heart

And we find John Ruthven back in favour
Ready to play his part.

The third Earl was a clever loon,
An educated man.
He studied the black arts in Italy
Afore he returned to this land.

But then for a' his cleverness
He did a stupid thing;
At Gowrie House in auld Perth toon
He tried tae haud the King.

Noo yince locked up by the Ruthven clan
King James could let pass by,
But a second time was a step too far,
It made his temper fly.

He called for help frae an upstairs room
And was rescued by his men;
John was stabbed an' his brither too –
They'd never nab him again.

So angry was the sovereign King
That once again they'd plotted,
Their bodies were tried in Edinburgh toon,
Then hung, drawn and quartered.

The Ruthven name was outlawed then
For ever from that hour;
The Place of Ruthven was renamed
Now called Huntingtower.

The Maiden's Leap

I was flushed, damp-faced and partly clad,
Held in the hard embrace of my lad;
Our passions burned, our heartbeats raced,
Forbidden fruits have the sweetest taste.

The pounding of blood in our veins gave way
To a sound on the stairs that made me say,
'Stop! No, don't! Stop! Hark! Don't kiss,
We cannot be found in your room like this.'

To be discovered – unthinkable fate,
His punishment – hard to contemplate;
So I grabbed my clothes and blew out the light
And slipped through the window, into the night.

And there on the roof in the breeze I stood,
The night air rapidly cooling my blood,
Gables and ledges of cold, hard stone
And slippery slates that the moon shone on.

The gap between one tower and the next
Was yawning and deep and I was vexed.
I'd often considered it during the day
And fancied it might be a possible way,

But now, in the darkness, it seemed so wide,
And me bare-footed, heart thumping inside.
I heard the hammering on my lad's door
So I jumped, hoping I'd make it o'er;

I soared through the air like an owl in flight,
My thin slip fluttering in the night
And landed – just! And without much grace,
But happy to be in a safer place.

My casement was open so I climbed through
And into my bed where I somehow knew
My sleepy eyes, full of innocence
Would easily count in a maid's defence.

But lying there trying to calm my heart
I knew that the only way to outsmart
My parents – the only thing we could do –
Was to leave this place and start anew.

And so to the Place of Ruthven, farewell!
No more in these side-by-side towers I'll dwell,
Whatever might lie in store past these gates,
We'll face it with love and embrace our fates.

HUNTLY

HUNTLY CASTLE IS a real show-off, stately palace; even in its present ruinous state this is easy to tell. If you look closely, you can see different phases of its development, from the 12th-century motte and bailey to the grand edifice constructed in the 16th century.

The Gordon family were, for a very long time, the most important, the wealthiest and the most powerful dynasty in the north-east of Scotland and the castle at Huntly (or Strathbogie, as it was previously known) reflected this. The 15th-century tower house was impressive enough but the castle was transformed around 1599 – when the Earls of Gordon were elevated to Marquesses – into something quite spectacular, evident not just in its scale, but in the fancy carvings and ornamentation of the frontispiece, the fireplaces and the south-facing exterior, with its oriel windows and proclamation carved in stone; all of these say 'this is the home of a very wealthy and powerful family'.

In the north-east corner of the castle courtyard are the side-by-side remains of the bakehouse and the alehouse. The number of family members, servants and staff must have been significant at the best of times and often swelled by visiting guests. In those days, people drank a lot of ale (it was safer than the water) and I guess bread was a staple part of the diet. I imagined that the bake-wife and alewife might have been close friends and that the bakehouse, with its continuously warm ovens, might have been an informal gathering place. This idea found expression through the words and musings of 'The Baxter Quine o' Huntly Castle'.

In 1556, Mary of Guise, who was Queen Regent at the time, visited George Gordon, the 4th Earl at Huntly. He was keen to show off his wealth, status, luxurious lifestyle and well-stocked stores. He may have tried too hard, for it is recorded that the French Ambassador who accompanied Mary of Guise advised her that this 'Cock o' the North' should maybe have his wings clipped. Clipped they eventually were, for although Mary of Guise died in 1560, her daughter, Mary Queen of Scots, confronted the upstart Earl in battle at Corrichie two years later. She may have felt that it was politically important to be seen to challenge and suppress Catholics who were growing bold and rebellious.

Gordon was defeated in the battle and taken prisoner, but then he fell from his horse and died. It seems that in those days it was not unusual for a dead man to stand trial for treason and that is exactly what happened to him. His eldest son, John, was also executed for good measure. The episode is recounted in 'The Battle of Corrichie Burn'.

There are many interesting things to see at Huntly Castle, and it is fun to imagine what it might have been like to live here, to own it even, in its days of glory. At the top of the main palace building is a small octagonal room called the belvedere (literally, a room with a good view). This must have been a cosy little place with a fire burning in the grate, remote from the hustle and bustle of the floors below and of course commanding stunning views. 'The Belvedere' describes what would have been my favourite retreat if I was the owner of Huntly Castle – a kind of man-cave in the sky.

The Baxter Quine o' Huntly Castle

In a corner o' Huntly Castle,
At the farthest end frae the Laird,
Are twa wee hooses side by side
Whaur the staples o' life are prepared.
In wan hoose the alewife's aye busy
Brewing her fine, tasty ale
And next door is me – the baxter quine:
Ah mak sure the Laird's breid's nivver stale.

Bannocks and banter and ale,
Bannocks, banter and ale,
Whatever the weather
You'll find us thegither,
The alewife next door and mysel'.

We baith get supplies frae the miller,
We baith tak' guid care o' oor yeast
And what we produce is the mainstay
O' breakfast or picnic or feast,
And though we hae muckle in common,
The grain and the grist and the barm,
The alehoose is no ayeweys comfy,
But ma hoose is constantly warm;
For Ah ha'e ma twa bakin' ovens,
Each yin like a beehive is walled
An' though they are frequently raked oot an' cleaned,
It's seldom that baith are stane cauld.
The alewife comes in for a crust
And she'll bring in a jug o' her ale,
So we sit in the warmth for a blether
And a moment o' rest frae travail;
Or sometimes she'll talk while Ah'm kneading,

Hair stuck tae ma heid wi' the sweat,
And it's then that her ale is maist welcome,
When Ah'm ower fashed an' ower het.

Bannocks and banter and ale,
Bannocks, banter and ale,
Whatever the weather
You'll find us thegither,
The alewife next door and mysel'.

A wheen o' folk work in the castle,
Some bide in, some sleep in the toon;
There's cooks and scullions and chamber maids,
Stable hands and store-cellar loons.
When it's quiet and dark in the winter,
If they canna find ingle or lum,
They'll tak' a wee trip tae the bakehoose
In search o' a heat and a crumb.
It's cosy late oan in the bakehoose,

Twa or three caunles gi'e licht;
We aye need fresh breid in the mornin'
So the ovens are working a' nicht.
There's no mony chairs in the bakehoose,
So the younger yins sit on the flair,
But the banter is guid an' the gossip an' a'
And some o' the tales – Ah declare!
We laugh and we sing an' tell stories,
Though ootside it may blaw a gale,
Twinklin' een and reid rosy cheeks
Frae the ovens and sma' draughts o' ale!

Bannocks and banter and ale,
Bannocks, banter and ale,
Whatever the weather
You'll find us thegither,
The alewife next door and mysel'.

The Laird and his Lady are human like us,
But they're born to a higher degree;
The world that they live in – the lives that they lead –
Seem unco and distant tae me.
But for a' their rare wines an' saft satins,
Wall-hangings and four-poster beds,
For a' their jewels an' knick-knacks
And fine powdered wigs oan their heads,
For a' their big books and fine learning
An' banquet feasts in the great hall,
For all their gold an' possessions
Ah dinna haud envy at a',
For ma life is uncomplicated
And Ah ha'e a' that Ah need,
The burdens Ah cairry are easy:
Mind the yeast – an' don't burn the breid!

Ah dinna ha'e power or siller,
There's a patch an' frayed sleeves oan ma goon,
But Ah've the best job in the castle,
Ah'm the luckiest quine in the toon.

Bannocks and banter and ale,
Bannocks, banter and ale,
Whatever the weather
You'll find us thegither,
The alewife next door and mysel'.

The Battle of Corrichie Burn

At Corrichie Burn on the Hill o' Fare
The Cock o' the North had his wings clipped sair,
At Corrichie Burn just by Meikle Tap
Gordon o' Huntly had his knuckles rapped.

Mary Queen o' Scots was a feisty quine,
She didnae hum and haw or mince her words;
As the female heid o' the Stuart line
She oft found her say-so was undermined
By rascally aristocrats and lords;
Yin day she'd be feted and wined and dined,
The next she'd be blamed and muckle-maligned;
Aye, it didnae tak' her long to find
That her lords were a scheming bunch o' turds.

The Earl o' Huntly was 'Cock o' the North',
A brazen birkie and a braggart loon,
A boastful bum who aye flaunted his worth
(The badge and the privilege of his birth)
Ower-endowed, baith in wealth and in girth
(His moo' had aye sooked oan a silver spoon).
Gain-stood by this bumptious and bold buffoon,
Queen Mary led an army north o' Perth.

At Corrichie Burn on the Hill o' Fare
The Cock o' the North had his wings clipped sair,
At Corrichie Burn just by Meikle Tap
Gordon o' Huntly had his knuckles rapped.

In the autumn o' fifteen sixty-two
The days were pleasant and the sky was blue –
But Huntly was facin' a hullaballoo.

The Earl, George Gordon, was noo in a huff;
He thought his clan had been rudely rebuffed
By the Queen (who was clearly far from chuffed)
And by that upstart scoundrel Earl o' Moray.
As tensions grew, the mair Huntly grew worried,
To risk his fine neck he was in nae hurry,
But he was in a fix, as well he knew.
His army marched eastwards to face the Queen
And Moray, who'd come ower frae Aberdeen.
At Corrichie Burn by the Hill o' Fare
The harsh sounds of battle soon rent the air,
Earl Gordon's fine swordsmen thrust, cut and slashed
But Moray's lang pikes they couldnae quite match;
And so Earl Huntly's ambitions were dashed
And his high hopes died on the hillside there.

At Corrichie Burn on the Hill o' Fare
The Cock o' the North had his wings clipped sair,
At Corrichie Burn just by Meikle Tap
Gordon o' Huntly had his knuckles rapped.

The hale Gordon clan was soon put to flight
And those that hadnae been captured were killed;
The burn ran red with the blood that was spilled;
Huntly was captured, then fainted with fright.
They said he was 'corpulent, short of breath –
And gross' – and so he tumbled aff his horse
And passed to the earthy embrace of death.
His sons, now moaning with noisy remorse,
Were huckled in chains off to Aberdeen;
The oldest, John, had but one night in bed
Before the keen Maiden took off his fine head.
The Queen from window above looking on
Shed many a tear for her bonnie John,

For a favourite of hers he once had been.
His father's body was wrapped and embalmed
And sent off by sea to Auld Reekie toon
To be tried for treason by Queen's command;
And 'guilty' the verdict was there written doon,
So Mary acquired his castles and land.

At Corrichie Burn on the Hill o' Fare
The Cock o' the North had his wings clipped sair,
At Corrichie Burn just by Meikle Tap
Gordon o' Huntly had his knuckles rapped.

The Belvedere

Up here, above it all;
I like coming here,
Heaven seems near
In this high belvedere –
My topmost room,
This is the crown,
The dome, my plume.
From here I look down,
Tracing the river
Winding forever;
Even tall trees seem small.

The calls and the cries
Of bustling lives
That I constantly hear
And that trouble me so
Are far down below –
Now dim and remote
And detached,
Out of reach,
Out of mind,
I leave that world behind;
When I come here I float
And deep peace I find
Here in my high belvedere.

I look out on the land
Over valley and hill,
At the apex I stand,
The zenith, the peak;
Such height gives a thrill
Quite unique.

As I gaze from my tower,
My high nest,
My bower,
It's like I can see
Almost everywhere;
I know I'm the highest;
There's nobody, anywhere,
Higher than me.

I climb to this place
To watch the sun rise
When I need to be wise
For the tasks that I face
And I watch the sun set
When I wish to reflect
And be grateful for grace,

For rest and repose,
To read or compose,
Or just to be on my own,
For sometimes a person
Can better determine
The right course
When he is alone.

And in the dark night
With a fire in the hearth,
I'm up here in the sky
In my eyrie so high;
When candles are lit
And soft shadows flit
I feel joy and delight,
Here in my favourite
Place on this earth.

LOCHLEVEN

LOCHLEVEN CASTLE'S POSITION, surrounded by water, makes it a difficult place to attack; it also makes it that little bit more complicated to visit. However, the effort is rewarded by a sense of peace and tranquil isolation greater than many other castles – a good place for contemplation.

The older parts of the castle, including the tower house and some of the curtain wall, date from around 1300. Such a stretch of time makes it more likely that interesting stories might be found in its past and I have drawn on three of these tales for material for my poems.

Taking them in chronological order, we start with a tale that involves William Wallace – and a conundrum. The Lochleven Castle guidebook says that, according to Blind Harry, Wallace and his men attacked the castle and slew its garrison of 30 men and five women. Reading my copy of *Blind Harry's Wallace*, however, I find this:

The inch they took boldly with sword in hand
And spared none before them that they fand
To wives and bairns he mercy still did show,
But thirty men upon the spot he slew.

Blind Harry also tells how the heroic Wallace swam across to the island in the middle of the night (wearing nothing but a sword around his neck) and rowed the castle boat back so that his 18 men could get to the island and attack the castle while the inhabitants were asleep. The poem 'Heroic Wallace' follows the account I found in *Blind Harry's Wallace*.

Moving on a few years, we find that in 1361 and 1362 King David II and his court stayed at Lochleven Castle hoping to avoid the dreaded Black Death, which was spreading northwards from England and may have caused the death of his wife, Queen Joan, in Hertford Castle in 1362. One imagines that the Black Death might have been a bit scarier in its day than Covid-19 has been to us.

The third poem, 'Young Willie Douglas', refers to the most famous episode in the castle's history – the imprisonment and eventual escape of Mary Queen of Scots. Mary was kept prisoner at Lochleven for 11 months in the care of Sir William Douglas, the castle's owner. She tried to escape a number of times and eventually succeeded with the help of William

Douglas, a young, orphaned kinsman of the castle's owner. The poem tells the story from young Willie's point of view. No doubt he was won over by Mary's charms, but it must have been quite an adventure for the lad, knowing the possibility of capture or the risk of retaliatory punishment later.

Heroic Wallace

The Wallace was scouring the Kingdom of Fife
To cleanse it of all English men;
He faced them and chased them in forest and moor
And thrashed them again and again.

One stronghold resisted The Wallace's hand,
Lochleven was hard to attack,
So he came to the loch in the dark of the night
For this was a nut he would crack.

He left all his followers safe by the fire
Enjoying good friendship and cheer,
He stripped off his clothes, strapped his sword to his back
And into the loch disappeared.

He swam to the island far out in the loch,
Like a selkie he clambered ashore;
He silently severed the boat from its tie,
Rowed back to his fellows once more.

The Englishmen slept in their strong island keep
Believing that they were secure,
But oh, what a fright they received that dark night
When The Wallace kicked in their door.

They ran to and fro just like mice in a nest
When that nest is broken apart,
Some in their nightshirts and some in their drawers,
Some still in the arms of sweethearts.

The Scots led by Wallace were running amok
For the blood lust blazed in their eyes

And though they were few, all the English they slew
And the castle they took as their prize.

That night on the isle thirty Englishmen died,
Thirty English who'd never go home,
But their bairns and their wives were granted their lives
For The Wallace said, 'Leave them alone.'

It's a long time ago and no-one can know
The events that really befell,
But thanks to the words of Blind Harry the bard
There's a story that we can retell.

Fleeing the Pest

It came from the south,
As all things with danger
And death seem to do;
The dark-hooded stranger
With thin evil mouth
And earth-tainted breath
Is carrying something for you.

This unwelcome guest
Has nothing to say,
But he carries the latest wave of the pest,
That fearsome mortality,
That gravest finality;
Those black seeds of death
He scatters and sows on his way.

When you wake in the light
Of a bright shining dawn,
Give thanks and give praise
For the sun's warming rays
And be sure to sup well
For you may soon be gone,
And though no-one can tell,
Your next breakfast might
Be taken in heaven or hell.

Some say it's the wages of sin,
The act of a God
Who does not spare the rod,
But punishes us for our ways.
He flogs us and flays
Us and brings up these lumps on our skin;
But other theories abound:

Some say it's caused by noxious smells
That seep up from under the ground,
Or that Jews may have poisoned the wells,
Or they look to the stars
And they find
That Jupiter, Saturn and Mars
In an ominous way are aligned.

It comes nearer each day
Like a dark locust swarm,
Like a winnowing wind
Sent to blow chaff away;
Or the biblical flood that took all those who'd sinned
Like a scythe through ripe corn;
Like a thatch catching fire
Will be quickly consumed –
We are all doomed,

For the Devil's reborn
And he's steadily coming this way.

Don't look to physicians
To find you a cure,
You'll just make them rich
And then you'll die poor;
There is no magician
Or wizard or witch
That can mend this condition,
It's something we must just endure.
There's nobody left to make ale or bread,
There's no-one to gather and bury the dead
And souls are in limbo,
For the cowardly priests
Who should have been giving us comfort at least,
Have locked up their doors and their windows
And fled.

This Black Death approaches – it's well on its way
And there must be more we can do than just pray
While waiting to die;
It's already struck home
For I hear that in England it's taken my Joan.
So I think we must fly,
And away to the north there's a place we might stay;
It's a castle that's built on an island remote
And the loch is its moat
And no-one can go there except by boat,
So let us go now and cut ourselves off,
For by crossing the loch
We can shield ourselves from exposure;
We might just find peace
In that pastoral place
And hope that this soon will pass over.

Young Willie Douglas

I pull on the oars and chew my lip,
Each pull and dip, each splash and drip,
Each slow and rhythmic, careful stroke,
Sounds like the strike of stone on oak;
No-one dares to stir or speak,
We wince with every thud and creak.

The night is like a cape of gloom,
We wish it darker than the tomb,
But a waxing toenail moon shines down
And dancing lights are all around.
With every sweep of slicing blade
The castle and the island fade
Into the distance and the past;
Our Queen is now set free at last.

A sudden owl disturbs the sky,
I hear its criminating cry;
It seems to ask the darkness, 'Who?'
And then replies, 'It's you, it's you!'
My heart beats like its wings with fear,
The castle still seems much too near;
I locked them in and took the keys,
But fate does not give guarantees.

The Queen, for whom I'm risking all,
Sits there wrapped in cloak and shawl,
Still and silent in gathered folds –
She wonders what the future holds
And I do fear for mine, but then
She's easier to love than bearded men.

STIRLING

STIRLING CASTLE IS just magnificent – one of those castles where a visitor might spend an entire day and still only scratch the surface; and it is so rich in stories, images and anecdotes that I could have written a whole volume of poems inspired by it.

Like Edinburgh Castle, it enjoys magnificent views from its walls and battlements perched on a commanding volcanic, rocky outcrop; it also dominates the landscape and can be seen from afar. Its strategic position, first point of crossing the River Forth which splits the country and at the threshold of the highland line, accounts for much of its historical importance, and for centuries it enjoyed a prestigious role as a royal residence and centre of the royal court. With so much royal influence and comings and goings, Stirling Castle is still a treasure trove of riches, displaying both the opulence of buildings and their furnishings and also the rich memories of historical adventures, intrigue and legend.

One of the cameos that always captured my imagination is the story of John Damian because it fascinated me that James IV would have employed an alchemist. Italian born Damian lived in the castle for five years; you have to wonder what James hoped to achieve by employing an alchemist – was it mainly about turning base metal into gold or did John Damian have other uses, for example producing alcoholic spirits or perfumes? Was he helpful to James in his political deliberations, in the same way that modern politicians engage shadowy figures with dodgy skills as advisers?

In 1507, perhaps in an attempt to refresh James's flagging interest in continuing to employ an alchemist who had actually achieved very little, Damian decided to impress his monarch by flying from the battlements of Stirling Castle – with France being his intended destination. Unsurprisingly, his attempt failed and he only avoided death by luckily landing on a midden (a heap of dung) below the castle. There have been other poetic accounts of Damian's foolhardy adventure, both sympathetic and unsympathetic. 'The Scottish Icarus' tries to tell the tale in some detail and with a little humour.

In previous visits to the castle, I have always enjoyed visiting the kitchens where a fabulous display has been created to show how the kitchen and its staff might have functioned in days gone by. On one or two occasions I was able to visit the tapestry studio and see some of the work being done to recreate a set of tapestries that tell the symbolic story of the hunting of the unicorn. I could not resist creating a suite of poems in tribute to this work and the finished tapestries, now on display in the palace of James V. My poems represent the stages of the hunt, finishing with 'The Unicorn in Captivity', which represents the resurrection and immortality of this mythical creature. In so many castles around Scotland we see the stone, but the soft furnishings and the artwork can only be imagined. Stirling Castle, with its furniture, wall paintings, Ceiling Heads (wooden carvings) and these tapestries, gives us a tantalising taste of life in one of the country's most important royal castles.

The Scottish Icarus

On this castle high, in days gone by, a wondrous thing occurred;
John Damian swore he would leap and soar and take to the air like a bird.
He'd gathered some fowls and eagles and owls and even a wren or two
And fashioned some wings with feathers and strings and sealing wax and glue.

He proudly displayed the wings he'd made to the court of good King James,
They fondled and stroked them, pulled at and poked them, not convinced of
   his claims,
But he swore he would soar up to heaven's door and over the clouds he'd dance
And in no time at all he would make landfall somewhere over in France.

Now John was a cad who quite clearly had many significant skills;
He held the position of royal physician and claimed he could remedy ills.
He played the best hand of cards in the land, as James soon found to his cost:
The King was dismayed that whenever they played for money, he always lost.

To the King he had sold the promise of gold, as alchemist to the court,
But before too long the King clocked on that he'd probably been sold short,
So when John declared he would fly like a bird, the sceptical King kept shtum,
For to weary James it was all the same – to France or to his doom.

So the day came round when John would astound the audience with his feat;
A small crowd came and so did James to witness John's conceit,
Standing on the edge of the battlement ledge with his bulky wings attached,
Like the head of a wren on the body of a hen or a fluffed-up cock, half-spatched.

His arms spread wide o'er the countryside, with the valley far below,
He tensed his muscles for the feathers ruffled as an updraft wind did blow;
He steadied his feet and started to beat the wings with his sweaty grip,
The crowd gave a gasp when the unsteady grasp of his sandals started to slip.

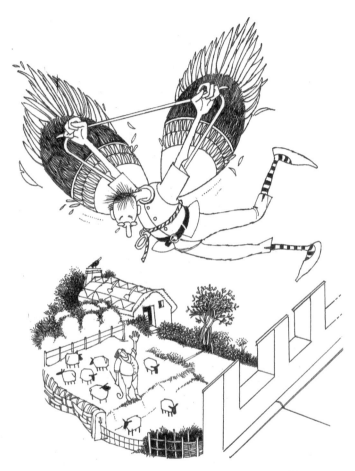

With a terrified squeal he rocked on his heels and thrust with all his might –
Forward he leapt as the up-rush swept and he spread his arms like a kite,
But his would-be flight was not like a kite – it was more like a falling stone:
He dived like a hawk, hit the castle rock – you could hear the crack of bone.

He bounced off there, back out into air, like a dead bird someone had flung
And far down below where tall grasses blow, he landed on a heap of dung.
Twisted with pain and trapped in his frame he sheepishly cast up a glance;
As James turned away, he was heard to say, 'I think he just landed in France!'

Hunting the Unicorn

I

The Start of the Hunt

Slowly I walked among forests and fields,
Through glades and shades where the sun never steals.
The thicket of thorns was tangled and dense;
We spread out like a fan, me and my friends,
Cross-combing the countryside, far and wide,
Seeking the place where the unicorn hides.
The unicorn is a creature of dreams
And quietly it drinks from clear, crystal streams;
I knew where such a stream tumbled and fell
And I lay there in wait, watching it well.
The day was drowsy and humming with flies,
The musical stream lulled sleep to my eyes.
All of a sudden my mind came awake
Surfacing out of its dark lily lake;
An arrow-thin sunbeam was shining on
The spectral white shape of a unicorn.
I climbed up a tree as soft as I could
And waved the hunters to come to the wood;
With smooth velvet garments and well-trained hounds,
I knew they would come without any sound.

II

The Unicorn is Found

The unicorn stood in the woodland glade,
Its innocence clearly beyond compare,
While silently hunters their ambush laid.
The unicorn stood in the woodland glade,
Not knowing the danger, quite unafraid,
Enjoying the peace and the beauty there;
The unicorn stood in the woodland glade,
Its innocence clearly beyond compare.

III

The Unicorn Leaps out of the Stream

Startled, the unicorn leaps from the stream,
Fleeing the danger she senses around,
Fleeing the grip of the killing machine,
Fleeing the hunters with horns and with hounds.

Arrows are flying, no place to hide,
Men wielding spears and the snarling of dogs;
Heart beating frantically, eyes staring wide,
She tries to escape but what are the odds?

Running in circles, the trap closing tight,
Blood on her body and fire in her head,
Kicking and stabbing she puts up a fight;
Finally conquered by panic and dread.

IV

The Unicorn at Bay

This beautiful forest has sunshine and shade
And water that gurgles in pure running streams,
The fruits of the forest are sweetly arrayed,
All nourished and fed by the sun's golden beams.

The glad woodland creatures all gambol and play
And scamper around among bushes and trees;
Look up and you might see a dove or a jay
And flowers are bright for the visiting bees.

The balance of nature is gently maintained,
It's neither too wild, nor yet too tamed;
Now nothing is perfect, that's easy to see,
But here there is beauty and sweet harmony;
The one thing that spoils Mother Nature's fine plan
Is hunting for sport – that's the footprint of man.

V

The Unicorn is Killed and Brought to the Castle

And so they killed the unicorn;
The hunter blew his bugle horn,
Around its neck they bound some thorns,
They laid it on a horse's back
And there it dangled, sad and slack,
Defeated, finished and forlorn.

The forest now has lost its cheer,
No happiness we'll see or hear,
The morning dew will taste of tears,
The woodland creatures now are sad
And all in shades of grey are clad;
The light they loved has disappeared.

The lords and ladies gather round
To see the creature dead and bound
And now like Christ with hawthorn crowned;
They think this proves them lords of all,
To hold the forest in their thrall;
Their playground now a battleground.

VI

The Unicorn in Captivity

The unicorn carries a light in its eyes
And though there are times when it flickers and fades,
Like dawn or the phoenix it always will rise.

When danger and thunderclouds darken the skies,
When enemies gather and seek to invade,
The unicorn carries a light in its eyes.

When threatened it runs and when injured it cries
But death is not something that makes it afraid;
Like dawn or the phoenix it always will rise.

Whatever it touches will be purified,
Wherever it wanders it banishes shade,
The unicorn carries a light in its eyes.

A king on whose banner the unicorn flies
May feel that his kingdom cannot be unmade;
Like dawn or the phoenix it always will rise.

So those who would capture her must realise,
Although they may threaten with bludgeon and blade,
The unicorn carries a light in its eyes
And like dawn or the phoenix it always will rise.

TANTALLON

THE AWESOME IMPRESSION made by Tantallon on many visitors owes something to the scale and formidable strength of its walls, towers and battlements, and perhaps even more to its location on a clifftop looking out over the Firth of Forth, the North Sea and the dramatic Bass Rock.

Its history is bound up with the fortunes, adventures and misadventures of the Douglas family: family feuds, odd marriages, power struggles with and treasonous plotting against the King, a role in the Rough Wooing and the early death of one Earl apparently because a witch cast a spell on him.

Tantallon survived a number of sieges, but for all its imposing power, it was no match for the artillery brought to bear upon it by Oliver Cromwell in 1651 and it was sufficiently damaged to necessitate surrender on that occasion. It was never rebuilt or properly inhabited after that date and had been largely left to decay until it was taken over by the state in 1924. The fact that it still stands so defiantly after more than 300 years of neglect shows how solidly it was built.

Marching from Dunbar towards Tantallon in 1528, the King's soldiers are said to have beat a march to the rhythm of 'Ding Doun Tantalloun'. Archibald Douglas, the 6th Earl, had married Queen Margaret, widow of James IV. This made him stepfather to the young King James V and he, perhaps unwisely, kept the young King prisoner in Edinburgh Castle for more than two years. In 1528, aged 17, James escaped and immediately retaliated by laying siege to Archibald in Tantallon. Despite their best efforts, over 21 days all the King's cannons and all the King's men could not make an impact on the castle walls and Archibald survived to hatch further treasonous plots in future years; I liked the idea of the army marching to Tantallon intent on bringing it down and sounding their advance with the drums.

Visiting Tantallon on a sunny summer day, I was taken with the view of the Bass Rock framed by one of the broken casements of the hall block and took a few photographs. The colours and the distance were entrancing, and gave rise to the sonnet 'View to the Bass Rock'.

Perhaps there may be some Freudian reason why I am drawn to peer down into the unseeable darkness of wells; 'The Tantallon Well' is just a reverie inspired by looking down into the depths of this well, which is one of the best preserved in any of the castles I have seen. It is fortunately covered by a safety grid, though I have wondered how many mobile phones might lie at the bottom of it.

Ding Doun Tantalloun

Ding doun Tantalloun,
Soon you'll hear the cannons boom;
Sturdy wa's will be cast doon,
Chattels scattered a' around.

Douglas is a glaikit loon,
A birkie and a daft buffoon,
He set his face against the croun
But soon he'll sing anither tune.

On oor way to Tantalloun
We picked up guns at Dunbar toon,
Lasses swoonin' in their goons,
Tae sodjers' charms they're no' immune!

Douglas is a brash baboon
And doitit tae, we must assume;
Noo Tantalloun will be his tomb
For we will doom him tae the gloom.

The michty wa's of Tantalloun
Oot o' solid stane are hewn,
But we'll inflict its mortal wound
An' leave it lying in a ruin.

Douglas thinks it's his cocoon,
But he has failed to read the runes;
Here comes a roch an' raw typhoon
That will his fortress sair impugn.

Ding doun Tantalloun,
For as the noon dispels the moon,
So these high wa's we will consume
And Dirty Douglas we'll ding doun.

View to the Bass Rock

Look – and through this shattered casement see
The outward, downward vista that's beyond;
The sky and sea are peppered white with gannets.

A perfect picture in hi-res 3D
(You can almost touch the far horizon)
Like looking through a telescope at planets.

Feel blithe, like some old Bass Rock escapee,
Your heart is lifted, flying on and on
Above the cold Bass Rock that once began its

Life as hot volcano. Your spirit's free
And somehow now you hold within your hand
A wand with which to banish earthbound sadness.

So much does this dark frame enhance the blue
And will forever hold this moment's view.

The Tantallon Well

Deep as eternity, deep as infinity,
Deep as the pit of despair,
Deep as the ocean where no light wins,
Deep as a cauldron to hold all sins
In the nethermost region of hell,
Deep and dark as your worst nightmare,
Deep as the Tantallon well.

No matter how often the sun comes up
Over the truculent waves,
Its light cannot penetrate there where the gloom
Is dark as a vampire's grave.

The best we can hope is that once in a while,
High in the sky overhead,
A moon might send down thin, silvery beams
To scatter the darkness and dread;

But who will be there to peep over the brim
When light hits the shadows below
And what will they see in the beam of the moon
Where white light and black waters flow?

For all the small coins that have ever been cast
Favour or luck to procure
And all the fierce dreams that did not come to pass
Lie deep in that darkness, obscure.

Deep as eternity, deep as infinity,
Deep as the pit of despair,
Deep as the ocean where no light wins,
Deep as a cauldron to hold all sins
In the nethermost region of hell,
Deep and dark as your worst nightmare,
Deep as the Tantallon well.

THREAVE

THREAVE CASTLE STANDS on an island in the river Dee, not far from the town of Castle Douglas. To visit, you must take a 15-minute walk from the car park and then summon the boat by ringing a bell; the boatman will come and take you over. This was my first visit to the castle, though I had previously visited Threave Gardens while on holiday in the area.

The tower house, though 650 years old, still impresses – at 30 metres high it is roughly equivalent to a ten-storey block of flats. It was built about 1370 by Archibald the Grim, Lord of Galloway, later to become the 3rd Earl of Douglas and one of the most powerful and important lords in the south of Scotland. Archibald was appointed Lord Warden of the Marches and was responsible for chasing the English out of Lochmaben Castle and back over the border, and for quelling the difficult Gallovidians; King David II was very grateful.

Archibald was nicknamed 'the Grim' by the English because of his fearsome, formidable countenance in the heat of battle, not because he was unattractive, though Walter Bower said, 'he was dark and ugly, more like a coco [a cook-boy] than a Noble'. Whatever the truth, I couldn't help playing with the name in the first poem, 'Overheard at Threave Castle'.

The second poem, 'Archibald the Grim is Late for his Tea' is likewise a bit frivolous, but also reflects on some of the many things which we take for granted now that would have been unknown in 14th-century Scotland. This is something I often think about when visiting our ancient castles – it makes you appreciate the relative ease and comfort of our way of life. Both poems make reference to Archibald's wife, Joanna de Moravia.

The Black Douglases were, ironically, quite a colourful crowd and William, the 8th Earl, was as colourful as any. He was the son of James Douglas who had presided over the Black Dinner in 1440. By murdering the young 6th Earl, James became the 7th Earl and then was succeeded in 1443 by William. William married Margaret (the Fair Maid of Galloway) who was his cousin and sister to the two boys his father had murdered in Edinburgh Castle.

One of the reasons why James II decided to stamp on the Black Douglases (as if that bull's head on the table were not enough) was because William, who had apparently been plotting against the King, had executed Patrick MacLellan of Bombie at Threave Castle, in defiance of James's instructions. This was perhaps the last straw and William Douglas paid dearly for it when he next met the King at Stirling Castle; defying the King in 14th-century Scotland was not a particularly smart move. The story is told in the poem 'Power Struggles'.

Overheard at Threave Castle

'Haw, Jeannie – here's a guy – Archibald the Grim!
How would ye fancy being mairriet to him?'

'Na, na, Winnie – Ah dinna think Ah wid,
Ah cannae imagine his manners wad be guid –
His personal hygiene wis probably rank
An Ah widnae be surprised at a' if he drank.'

'But he wis a nobleman – never mind the grim,
This castle, and others, belanged tae him.
You could be the lady o' a' this land,
Hoity toity, posh and grand!'

'Aye that sounds fine when you pit it like that,
But what if he was ugly or smelly or fat?
What if he wis a grumpy-faced auld curmudgeon?
Ah might end up in the castle dungeon;
If Ah didnae dae as Ah wis telt
Ah might get laldy aff his leather belt.'

'But he wis Lord o' Galloway – an important man
And Earl o' Douglas – a famous clan.
He chased the English back ower the border
An' kept the March in proper order.'

'Ahh – but Lords back then – they were ayeways schemin'
He micht ha'e been a Machiavellian demon.
Ah ask ye – Jumpin' Jehoshaphat,
Whae'd want tae marry a bloke like that?'

'Weel he micht ha'e had a touch o' a megalomania,
But it says he mairriet Joanna de Moravia
And wad ha'e focht five knights for her hand;
Sounds like a romantic firebrand!'

'Huh! If he kent her real name wis just Joan Murray
He micht no ha'e been in sic a hurry
An' it says he wis 'dark an' ugly like a coco';
Tae mairry him Ah'd ha'e tae be loco.
Na – Ah'm mair the kind tae mairry for love,
Which is hoo Ah got the penniless waster that Ah huv!'

Archibald the Grim is Late for his Tea

Come boatman, let us cross the Dee,
Joanna is preparing tea,
We have no kettle, no TV,
No microwave or fridge –
They have not been invented yet –
But worst of all we have no bridge
And I mustn't get my tunic wet.

So come now boatman, please make haste,
I'm starved and have no time to waste,
The river runs in heavy spate
And for my tea I can't be late.
Joanna is the maid of Moray
And for her sake I have to hurry;
I wonder what she'll serve for tea?
I know what stuff I will not get –
Turkey, corn or avocado,
No pecan pie or sweet potato,
No pizza pie or kedgeree
Or chocolate cake – no way! Not yet!

Come on now boatman, pull those oars,
Forget your blisters, hacks and sores,
If Englishmen were in pursuit
I bet you'd pull them like a brute.
I fear my tea is getting cold,
I'll feel Joanna's stranglehold –
But wait! You must think me demented
For tea has not yet been invented;
So many things we've yet to see,
Let's hope that they will come to be –
And I will make a special plea;
A bridge for me to cross the Dee.

Power Struggles

Patrick MacLellen of Bombie
Was cast in the prison at Threave,
William the eighth Earl of Douglas
A dastardly plan had conceived

To join with some other high nobles
In order to challenge the King,
But Patrick was loyal to James
And would not support such a thing.

Lord Andrew Gray came to Douglas,
A letter from James in his hand,
To liberate Patrick MacLellan
Was King James's royal command.

The Douglas prevaricated,
Lord Gray was invited to dine;
The Earl said he'd open the letter
Once they had taken some wine,

But while they both sat at the table
Sharing the meat and the bread,
Sir Patrick was dragged from the prison
And quickly relieved of his head.

'Oops!' said the wily Earl Douglas
As soon as the letter he read,
'I'm sorry, but you are too late;
Sir Patrick is already dead.'

Thus did the scheming Earl Douglas
Display his contempt for the crown
And James who was seething with anger
Summonsed him to Stirling town;

They quarrelled and then it turned nasty:
James called the Douglas a brute,
The Earl got it right in the neck
And was defenestrated to boot!

So now we can unpick the lesson;
You must choose your battles with care,
Prepare for your meetings with caution
And beware lest you're caught in a snare.

URQUHART

THIS IS ANOTHER complicated castle, built and rebuilt in various stages since its early Pictish incarnation as a hill fort, then into the first stone castle built by the Durwards in the early 13th century, some later additions by John Comyn and then a major remodelling by the Grant family sometime in the 1500s.

The earliest written reference to Urquhart is in St Adomnán's *Life of St Columba*. It seems that St Columba visited here around 580AD, converting and baptising local chiefs on his travels. He also converted the Loch Ness Monster from ravening, man-eating beast to terrified water snake just by making the sign of the cross in the air and giving the monster a telling off. This might explain why Nessie has been so reluctant to show herself ever since, even near Urquhart Castle which must be the best monster-viewing spot on the whole of Loch Ness. 'The Explanation' is my story of a possible sighting of the monster in recent times.

The history of Urquhart Castle is that of the usual rise and fall of lordships and dynasties, of shifts in power and fortune connected both to local and to national events, from the Wars of Independence to the struggles between the Scottish kings and the Lords of the Isles, and later on the various Jacobite uprisings. It was the Jacobite rebellion of 1689 that ended this castle's period as a fortification of any military importance; government troops blew up the gatehouse when they left in 1692 – the evidence is still there to view.

Many of these events and adventures are only sketchily recorded and of course the more tranquil, domestic phases in-between are even less likely to be documented. One episode that was written down in some detail was the Great Raid of 1545 by the MacDonalds of Clanranald. The record contains an impressive list of things taken and their value – perhaps it was the evidence for an insurance claim. In any case, it seems to squeal loudly with indignation and anger, and I have tried to capture these feelings in 'The MacDonalds' Takeaway'.

The third poem, 'The Two Chambers', was written after reading one of the information boards near the castle visitor centre, which mentions a legend of two secret rooms under the castle – one of which contains vast treasure and gold, while the other contains only the plague. One of the tour guides advised me, with a conspiratorial wink, that there are indeed vaults under the great hall that have never been properly explored or excavated; so you never know – it may be more than just a fanciful legend.

The Explanation

Ah sat doon by the shore o' Loch Ness
No far frae old Drumnadrochit,
Wi' a Monster Mash beer in ma gless
An' ma drooth wis vera near slockit,
But no quite.

Ma square-slice wis het oan the grill,
The rolls an' the broon sauce stood ready,
Ah hud a few minutes tae kill
So Ah popped aff anither wee bevy;
Oan the skyte!

Ah could see Urquhart Castle nearby
An' the hills were a' bonnie wi' heather,
A bright shining sun in the sky
An' a beer tae cool the warm weather;
'Twis jist right!

Ah heard a splash oot oan the loch
An' Ah thocht 'the salmon are jumpin''
But when Ah turnt roond Ah wis wrocht
An' ma hert wis leapin' an' thumpin';
Whit a fright!

Ah stertit in shock and in awe,
Straight at me breinged a great monster,
Nae catfish or big eel this – naw,
This wis a richt heckin' chonker;
Ah went white!

This thing wis the size o' a hoose,
A truly fantastical species,
Ah could feel a' ma innards go loose,
Ah wis quakin' wi' they heebie-jeebies;
Holy shite!

Its een had the glare o' a deil
An' a moothfu' o' fangs sherp as daggers,
Ah niver thocht monsters were real –
Inventions o' liars an' braggarts;
Ah'm contrite!

It gi'ed me a shrivellin' stare
An' roared like thunder an' lightnin',
Ah wis filled wi' fear an' despair,
Ah've niver seen naethin sae fright'nin'
In ma life!

Ah thocht that ma time had run oot,
To fortune yin last time a hostage,
But it seemed Ah wis aff the hook;
It swallaed ma square-slice Lorne sausage
In wan bite!

It turnt and knocked me tae the flair,
Gaed back tae the loch at full throttle
And that's how Ah'm here oan the shore,
Unconscious, surrounded by bottles;
So there – an' Ah wish ye goodnight!

The MacDonalds' Takeaway

Along the shore, at misty close of day,
The beady-eyed MacDonald magpies came;
The watch was sleeping and should bear the blame,
But for his failing he's already paid.
They breached the water gate and surged inside
So what else could we do but run and hide?

They must have known the master was away
(They sniff and skulk and sneak about the land)
And when the master mouser's not at hand,
Then thieving, rustling rats come out to play;
So we were caught off-guard and ill-prepared,
Like hapless rabbits in the hunter's snare.

They plundered loot from every castle neuk,
Each storeroom, cellar, kitchen, pantry, stable,
All ransacked by this boist'rous, uncouth rabble,
As anything they saw and liked, they took;
They filled their boats and then filled ours as well
And all they left behind – their rancid smell.

They took bed covers and they took the beds,
Our pots and pans and kettles they purloined
And all that they could find of gold or coin;
They scoffed our ale and scranned our meat and bread
And what they couldn't batter down their throats
They stuffed away for later in their boats.

Like seagulls when the fishing fleet comes in,
They glugged our wine and tried on ladies' frocks,
They stole the doors and even took the locks,
All tools and weapons gone – each brooch and pin;

Our winter store of precious sacks of grain;
Two serving maids were never seen again.

They left some men behind to take our herds,
They gathered sheep and goats from all the land,
Our fine black cattle too they now command;
They even robbed the doocot of its birds
And like black vultures they would not go home
Till the carcass had been picked to the bone.

The Two Chambers

Beneath these crumbling walls a secret lies,
A story half-recalled from ancient times;
Two chambers, both the same in shape and size,
Though inside, very different things you'll find.
It's said that one's a treasure trove of gold,
Enough to make you rich for evermore,
But that's not what the other chamber holds,
For plague and death await behind that door.
And should you find these rooms you could not tell
Which one contains the gold and which the pest;
One door might lead to heaven, one to hell,
But who would be prepared to take the test?
When man takes risks great wealth to gain
He often finds that all he wins is pain.

ACKNOWLEDGEMENTS

I WOULD LIKE to thank Gavin Mac-Dougall of Luath Press for agreeing to indulge me in my departure from my usual subject of whisky, in spite of his suspicion that poetry and crumbling castles may not have quite the broad appeal that whisky seems to have these days.

Bob Dewar has also stayed with me on my journey to this new subject matter and I appreciate his illustrations and once again acknowledge his genius.

I owe a tremendous debt to my mother-in-law, Edith Ryan; firstly for the membership of Historic Environment Scotland that she gifted our family and secondly for her example and encouragement in helping me to move from my usual craft of composing songs to the less familiar task of writing naked verses of poetry (no melody to hide behind).

I appreciate the company I have often enjoyed while visiting these castles – especially my wife, Ursula, and our children and also various friends. I thank them for their patience, in case I may have tarried too long occasionally, while soaking up the atmosphere and sniffing out stories.

Lastly I acknowledge my debt to Historic Environment Scotland and the wonderful job they do in looking after these buildings. I have greatly appreciated the professionalism, enthusiasm and knowledge that I frequently encountered from the guides and other employees during these visits. Their official souvenir guide books and other publications have also been immensely helpful in clarifying some of the very complicated facts and fables associated with the castles in their care.

Luath Press Limited

committed to publishing well written books worth reading

LUATH PRESS takes its name from Robert Burns, whose little collie Luath (*Gael.*, swift or nimble) tripped up Jean Armour at a wedding and gave him the chance to speak to the woman who was to be his wife and the abiding love of his life. Burns called one of the 'Twa Dogs' Luath after Cuchullin's hunting dog in Ossian's *Fingal*. Luath Press was established in 1981 in the heart of Burns country, and is now based a few steps up the road from Burns' first lodgings on Edinburgh's Royal Mile. Luath offers you distinctive writing with a hint of unexpected pleasures.

Most bookshops in the UK, the US, Canada, Australia, New Zealand and parts of Europe, either carry our books in stock or can order them for you. To order direct from us, please send a £sterling cheque, postal order, international money order or your credit card details (number, address of cardholder and expiry date) to us at the address below. Please add post and packing as follows: UK – £1.00 per delivery address; overseas surface mail – £2.50 per delivery address; overseas airmail – £3.50 for the first book to each delivery address, plus £1.00 for each additional book by airmail to the same address. If your order is a gift, we will happily enclose your card or message at no extra charge.

Luath Press Limited
543/2 Castlehill
The Royal Mile
Edinburgh EH1 2ND
Scotland
Telephone: 0131 225 4326 (24 hours)
Email: sales@luath.co.uk
Website: www.luath.co.uk